Casseroles
I have known

A KEY-WORD BOOK

Casseroles
I have known

Compiled by

Flo Price

Word Books, Publisher—Waco, Texas

A KEY-WORD BOOK
Published by Pillar Books
For Word Books, Publisher

First Printing—April 1973
Second Printing—May 1974
First Paperback Printing—April 1976
  Second Paperback Printing—May 1977

CASSEROLES I HAVE KNOWN
Copyright © 1973 by Word, Incorporated
Waco, Texas 76703

Library of Congress catalog card number: 72-96354
ISBN: 0-87680-868-2
Printed in the United States of America

Grateful acknowledgment is made for permission to reprint the following copyrighted material: Quotations from *The Many Faces of Love* by Lois Fiedler. Copyright © 1968 by Fleming H. Revell Company, used by permission. Quotations from *I've Got to Talk to Somebody, God* by Marjorie Holmes. Copyright © 1968, by Marjorie Holmes Mighell. Reprinted by permission of Doubleday & Company, Inc.

Cover photo by Peggy Zarnek, Photo Ideas, Chicago, Illinois.

*To my mom and my friend "Ted" Kleeves,
who has taught me so much more than how
to cook, and to my lovely daughter Melody,
whom I have tried to teach some of the
things my mother taught me*

*Thanks to my great friend Gwen Waggoner,
whose dazzling skill on the typewriter has
saved my "hunt and peck" fingers from long
hours of forced labor*

Contents

Meat

Unexpected Company

They'll be here soon, the company I wasn't expecting and really don't want very much—but thank you for them.

Bless this house (and help me to get it cleaned up in time). This kitchen (and help me to find in it something worthy of guests).

Bless my dear foolish husband who invited them, and me as I strive to be a good hostess and a good wife to him.

Bless this table that I'm preparing; these linens (thank you that they're clean); this china and silver, these candles, wobbly though they are. This room, this meal—may it all turn out to be shining and good and lovely, to compensate for my sense of distress, ill humor, of not wanting to bother.

Oh, Lord, thank you for these guests as they drive toward us (and make them drive slowly, please).

I send out thoughts of love toward them, I send out welcome, and these thoughts ease my nervousness and make me genuinely glad inside.

Thank you for their friendship. Thank you that they have called us and can come. Thank you for the greetings and the news and the ideas that we will exchange.

Fill us all with rejoicing. Make us feel your presence among us. Bless our coming together in the warm hospitality of my house.

Marjorie Holmes

BEEF BRAISED IN SOUR CREAM

3½-4 lb. chuck roast
½ cup (1 stick) butter
1 pint whipping cream, not
   whipped

2 cloves garlic, minced
¼ cup lemon juice
1½ teaspoons salt
¾ teaspoon pepper

Roast chuck roast until done. Cool and slice. Make sauce of rest of ingredients and boil for about 3 minutes. Pour half of sauce in pan. Put slices of meat in pan and cover with rest of sauce. Bake at 350 degrees for 15 minutes.

Mary Ruth (Mrs. Don) Shadrick, Valparaiso, Indiana

I begged this recipe from Mary Ruth a couple of years ago, and it has been one of my very favorites in my recipe file. (Good cooks seem to run in her family. Her mom is a great cook too!) Mary Ruth teaches school, is homemaker and mother of two darling children.

STEAK ITALIANO

2 lbs. chuck steak, 1 inch
   thick, cut into serving
   pieces
1 envelope Lipton onion
   soup mix
1 1-lb. can Italian peeled
   tomatoes

1 teaspoon oregano
Freshly ground pepper and
   garlic powder to taste
2 tablespoons cooking oil
2 tablespoons wine vinegar

In large skillet, arrange meat; cover with onion soup mix and tomatoes. Sprinkle with oregano, pepper, garlic powder, oil, and vinegar. Simmer, covered, 1½ hours or until meat is tender. Makes 4 to 6 servings.

TROPICAL STEAK

What a lovely thing to do to sirloin steak—"tropicalize" it! If you're an avocado fiend like I am, you'll have to try this one fast. Try wearing a grass skirt when you serve it for added effect. (Smile)

2 lbs. round or sirloin steak, cut into ½-inch strips	2 medium onions, sliced thin ½ cup water

Brown steak. Add onions and water. Cover and simmer 30 minutes.

½ cup brown sugar 2 tablespoons vinegar 2 tablespoons cornstarch	⅓ cup soy sauce ½ teaspoon ground ginger ⅔ cup pineapple juice

Mix above ingredients together in saucepan. Cook until thick. Add to meat.

1 can mushrooms 2 fresh tomatoes, skinned and cut into 8ths	1 large can pineapple chunks 1 medium avocado, peeled and cut into ½-inch strips

Fold above ingredients into meat mixture and heat. Serve over fluffy rice. Serves 6.

Pauline (Mrs. Gil) DeHamer, Wheaton, Illinois

Thanks to Pauline, wife of Gil DeHamer, vice president of marketing and sales for Christian Life magazine.

EASY BEEF STROGANOFF
With an Elegant Air

1 lb. fresh mushrooms, sliced 1 cup onion, sliced fine 5 tablespoons butter	4 tablespoons catsup 2 10½-oz. cans condensed beef bouillon

2 lbs. fillet of beef, cut into
    very thin strips
2 teaspoons salt
Sprinkling of paprika
2 cloves garlic, minced

⅓ cup flour (generous)
1 pint sour cream
8 cups cooked wild rice
1 10-oz. pkg. frozen peas,
    cooked (optional)

Prepare day or two in advance. Sauté mushrooms and onions in butter until onion is tender. Remove from fry pan. Set aside. Brown meat quickly in same pan. Add salt, paprika, garlic, catsup, and bouillon to the meat. Cover and simmer no more than 15 minutes. Add flour to some liquid from pan. Stir into meat mixture. Add onions and mushrooms. Mix. Heat until bubbly and thickened while stirring constantly. Refrigerate.

Before serving, heat meat mixture with sour cream. Serve on bed of wild rice or in ring of wild rice mixed with peas. Serves 10. Lovely served with a tossed green salad.

Harriet (Mrs. Kenneth) Smith, Greenwich, Connecticut

Harriet Smith enjoys sailing, and says she has prepared "vast numbers of meals in the galley of the Currensea at various precarious degrees of heat." She suggests we make her stroganoff in a nice quiet, stable kitchen! Harriet is active in various forms of Christian work. Her husband, Ken, does a great deal of preaching and is president of his company, United States Banknote Company.

EASY CASSEROLE

1 cup elbow macaroni
1 10½-oz. can condensed
    cream of mushroom soup
1 cup milk
1 cup grated cheese (long-
    horn or cheddar)

1 tablespoon chopped onion
½ tablespoon parsley flakes
1 pkg. sliced smoked beef
    (can substitute tuna or
    chicken)

Cook macaroni according to package directions.

Combine all ingredients in a greased casserole. (I use a flat casserole and cut into squares to serve.) Refrigerate overnight. Cover with foil and bake at 350 degrees for 45 minutes. Uncover and brown for 10–15 minutes. Serves 6. (Can serve with a white sauce with mushrooms, or cream of celery soup with pimentos spooned over the top of each serving.)

Phyllis (Mrs. Covell J.) Hart, Deerfield, Illinois

Phyllis Hart is a clinical psychologist who works for the Department of Mental Health of the state of Illinois. She is married to Covell Hart, who is a Presbyterian minister. Together they work in small groups, Bible study groups, and in dialogue preaching.

GROUND BEEF-NOODLE CASSEROLE

Lois Linkletter has a last name that is almost a household word, being the wife of Art Linkletter, radio and television personality. She is known for her interior decorating skills and is an exceptional weaver. Lois sent not only a casserole recipe, but a whole dinner menu which is a family favorite! She is one of those good cooks who doesn't measure things (a pinch of this and a dash of that!) but says everyone can proportion the following ingredients to his (or her) own taste:

Ground beef	Garlic
Noodles	Bell pepper
Tomato paste	Chopped black olives
Water	Chopped pimentos
Onions	Whole kernel canned corn

She serves this tasty dish with garlic toast, spiced pears, and a salad of very thinly sliced cucumbers in marinade. For dessert she serves lemon or lime ice.

Lois (Mrs. Art) Linkletter, Beverly Hills, California

PIONEER CASSEROLE

2 lbs. boneless beef stew meat,
    cut in 1-inch cubes
3 tablespoons lard or drip-
    pings
1 teaspoon salt
¼ teaspoon pepper
½ cup chopped onion
2 teaspoons Worcestershire
    sauce

1 cup water
1 10½-oz. can condensed
    cream of mushroom soup
1 10½-oz. pkg. frozen peas
    and carrots
1½ cups homemade biscuit
    mix (or Bisquick), liquid
    added
1 teaspoon parsley flakes

Brown meat in lard or drippings. Pour off drippings. Add salt, pepper, onion, Worcestershire sauce, and water. Cover tightly and simmer 2 hours, or until meat is tender. Add soup, peas and carrots. Cover tightly and cook slowly for 10 minutes. Place hot mixture in 6 individual casseroles. Combine parsley flakes and biscuit mix. Drop ⅓ cup dough over each casserole. Bake in a hot oven, 400 degrees, 20 to 25 minutes or until brown. Serves 6.

Trish Lenihan, Kansas City, Missouri

Wouldn't you expect a dish like Pioneer Casserole from a really and truly cowgirl and former rodeo queen? Trish Lenihan is a national representative for Stonecroft Ministries (Christian Women's Clubs and Christian Business and Professional Women), and travels across the country singing (great voice) and sharing her faith in Christ. She says she grew up "on the back of a horse," and still loves to go home to her dad's Hereford ranch in North Dakota to "punch" cows! We've enjoyed having Trish as a guest in our home. (I think the only reason she came was because we had horses!)

BEEF NOODLE CASSEROLE

2½ cups noodles
3 tablespoons melted marga-
    rine

½ teaspoon monosodium
    glutamate
1½ lbs. ground beef

1-lb. carton cottage cheese
6 oz. cream cheese and chives
⅓ cup thick sour cream
½ cup minced onion
2 tablespoons chopped green pepper
1 small jar pimento
½ teaspoon salt

3 8-oz. cans tomato sauce
Few drops Tabasco sauce
½ teaspoon parsley
½ teaspoon salt (for meat)
½ teaspoon Worcestershire sauce
½ teaspoon paprika

Cook noodles, drain, and blend in 3 tablespoons margarine. Set in warm place. Mix together cottage cheese, cheese and chives, sour cream, onion, green pepper, pimento, salt, monosodium glutamate. Set aside.

Brown meat; drain off fat. Stir in tomato sauce, Tabasco, parsley, salt, Worcestershire sauce and paprika.

Pour ½ meat mixture on bottom of casserole, ½ noodles, all of cheese mixture, other half of noodles and top with remaining half of meat sauce. Bake 50 to 60 minutes at 350 degrees. You may use two pounds of ground beef if desired.

Evelyn (Mrs. Oral) Roberts, Tulsa, Oklahoma

Evelyn Roberts, charming and gracious wife of the Reverend Oral Roberts, shares this word about her special interests: "For several years my special interest has been my husband's work. I enjoy taking part in whatever he does, although I prefer to stay in the background instead of being out in front. I have done much traveling with him all over the world and have met so many wonderful people. Occasionally, I accept a speaking engagement, when it doesn't conflict with my husband's schedule."

LAURA LEE'S TWO-CHEESE CASSEROLE

1 pkg. of noodles
2 lbs. ground beef
1 1-lb. carton cottage cheese
1 8-oz. pkg. cream cheese

1 onion, chopped (or several green onions, chopped, make it even better)
½ green pepper, chopped

1 pint sour cream | 1 or 2 8-oz. cans tomato sauce
| Salt and pepper to taste

Cook noodles according to package directions. Drain well. Brown ground beef. Set aside. Mix together cheeses, sour cream, onion, and green pepper.

Put half of noodles in large, flat casserole. Spread all of cheese mixture evenly over noodles. Top with remaining half of noodles, and cover with cooked ground beef. Pour 1 or 2 cans tomato sauce over entire mixture. Season with salt and pepper to taste. Bake at *low* temperature, about 300 degrees, until heated through (approximately 1 hour). This is also good reheated. (I hope your husband isn't picky about leftovers!)

Laura Lee (Mrs. Doug) Oldham, Lynchburg, Virginia

Laura Lee was very modest about her own accomplishments but, among other things, I know she must be a good cook and a good traveler. Her husband is popular gospel singer and recording artist, Doug Oldham.

LASAGNE FOR 24

Mary says this lasagne recipe is one of Jim's favorite dishes.

3 lbs. ground beef
1 lb. ground pork, fresh
2 cups chopped onion
2 garlic cloves, minced
2 large cans (1 lb. 12 oz. each) tomatoes
2 15-oz. cans tomato sauce
2 teaspoons salt
3 tablespoons sugar
3 tablespoons parsley flakes
2 teaspoons crushed basil

2 2-lb. cartons creamed small curd cottage cheese
1 cup grated Parmesan cheese
2 tablespoons parsley flakes
2 teaspoons salt
2 teaspoons crushed oregano
1 lb. lasagne noodles, cooked and drained
1½ lbs. shredded mozzarella cheese
1 cup grated Parmesan cheese

Cook and stir ground beef, pork, onions, and garlic in roaster or heavy kettle until meat is browned and onion tender. Drain off fat and add tomatoes. Break tomatoes up with fork. Stir in tomato sauce, salt, sugar, parsley flakes, and basil. Simmer uncovered one hour or until mixture thickens. Heat oven to 350 degrees.

Mix cottage cheese, 1 cup Parmesan cheese, 2 tablespoons parsley flakes, 2 teaspoons salt and oregano. In two oblong pans, 13 x 9½ x 2, layer half each of drained noodles, sauce, mozzarella cheese, and cottage cheese mixture. Repeat, reserving enough sauce to cover the top with a thin layer. Spread sauce over top and sprinkle with 1 cup Parmesan cheese.

Bake uncovered for 45 minutes. Allow additional baking time if casserole has been made ahead of time and refrigerated. After removing from oven, let stand 15 minutes before serving.

Note from Flo: If you're going to go to all this trouble, I really think you *should* have company! If you're just making it for the family or a smaller group, cut recipe in half. It's even *better* warmed up the next day.

Mary (Mrs. James) Irwin, Denver, Colorado

During a recent visit to the Houston Space Center to do some filming for the Treehouse Club television program, Astronaut Colonel Jim Irwin took us on a guided tour through the center. Among other things, I got to climb up into the LEM (Lunar Excursion Module) for pictures, which was really a thrill! The next day Jim took me on a "guided tour" through his home where I met his pretty wife, Mary, and two of his four children. Mary is a talented artist, and several of her paintings grace the walls of their home. Jim has begun a new gospel ministry called High Flight, Inc.

Italian Spaghetti

Billie Barrows says: "It seems that almost every time I serve this, someone asks for the recipe. This to me is always the 'proof of the pudding.' It is more 'special' than just plain spaghetti and easy to fix and serve."

2 tablespoons bacon fat
1 large onion, chopped
1 green pepper, chopped
2 lbs. lean ground beef
1 large can tomatoes
1 10¾-oz. can condensed
tomato soup
1 small can chopped mush-
rooms

1 bud garlic, finely chopped
1 teaspoon Worcestershire
sauce
1 bottle chili sauce
½ cup sliced pimento stuffed
olives
1 8-oz. package spaghetti
Grated cheese

Sauté chopped onion and green pepper in bacon fat until tender. Add meat and brown. Add tomatoes, tomato soup, mushrooms, and garlic. Cook about 40 minutes; then add Worcestershire sauce, chili sauce, and sliced olives.

Cook spaghetti (break spaghetti in half) in salted water until almost tender. Drain and mix with sauce. Put in large casserole and top with grated cheese. Put in oven for 10–15 minutes at 350 degrees. Serves 8. We like this with just a tossed salad and garlic bread.

Billie (Mrs. Cliff) Barrows, Greenville, South Carolina

Billie Barrows loves to entertain and to cook. She says she especially likes to try new recipes. (Here's a whole bookful for you, Billie!) She enjoys playing the piano and playing tennis and is a counselor for Christian Women's Club in Greenville. Billie also delights in going antique-hunting for primitive pine pieces for their mountain home. Her husband, Cliff Barrows, has been an outstanding member of the Billy Graham team for several years.

MANICOTTI

1 lb. manicotti noodles
2 lbs. ground round beef
½ teaspoon garlic salt
2 tablespoons chili powder

½ teaspoon paprika
Salt and pepper
1 lb. longhorn cheese, grated
2 large bottles Ragú spaghetti
sauce

Boil noodles until tender. Brown meat and add seasonings. Add half the grated cheese and stuff noodles with this mixture. Place noodles in baking dish, and pour over Ragú sauce (which has been heated). Sprinkle remaining grated cheese on top of sauce. Cover with foil and bake at about 300 to 325 degrees for 45 minutes.

Maude Aimee (Mrs. Rex) Humbard, Akron, Ohio

Even though this is Maude Aimee Humbard's specialty, her daughter Elizabeth also had a hand in sharing it with us. When her mom was running a little behind schedule, I wrote to Liz and asked her if she could help. (Is that sneaky??!) Liz came through as her mother's "very personal secretary" and sent us our recipe. Despite a grueling schedule of travel and personal appearances, Maude Aimee always manages to look fresh and lovely. (Since we do our television programs for Treehouse Club at Cathedral Teleproductions, I'm able to visit with the Humbards quite often during taping.) God is really blessing this unusual television ministry in which the entire family has a part.

ITALIAN CASSEROLE

I happen to know that Lois is not Italian, but she makes a great Italian casserole!

1 16-oz. pkg. elbo roni	1 cup cottage cheese
1½ lbs. ground beef	1 8-oz. pkg. cream cheese
3 8-oz. cans tomato sauce	1 cup sour cream
1 tablespoon Italian season- ing	⅓ cup chopped green onion
1 tablespoon garlic salt	2 tablespoons finely chopped green pepper
2 tablespoons parsley flakes	3 tablespoons melted butter
Salt and pepper to taste	

Cook elbo roni according to package directions. Brown ground beef. Add tomato sauce, Italian seasoning, garlic salt, parsley flakes, salt and pepper to taste. Set aside.

Combine cottage cheese, cream cheese, sour cream, onion,

and green pepper. Layer elbo roni and cheeses starting with elbo roni and finishing with it. Pour butter over top. Spread ground beef sauce mixture on top. Garnish for eye appeal. Bake at 350 degrees for 45 minutes. Serves 8–12.

Lois (Mrs. Bob) Daniels, Garden Grove, California

Lois is administrative assistant at LaHabra Fashion Square of LaHabra, California, and is organist and director of choral music at Norwalk Community Church, Norwalk, California. She is the wife of Bob Daniels, well-known recording artist and radio and television announcer.

TAGLIARINI

1 medium onion, chopped
2 tablespoons shortening
1 lb. ground round steak (or chuck)
1 10¾-oz. can condensed tomato soup
1 can water
1 cup uncooked fine noodles
1 can Mexicorn (or 1 can corn and chopped green pepper)
Salt to taste
Dash each: black pepper
oregano
thyme
basil
1 cup grated cheese

Brown onion in shortening; then brown ground steak. Add tomato soup and water. Add noodles and cook until tender. Mix in mexicorn, seasonings, and some of the cheese. Sprinkle rest of cheese on top. Bake at 350 degrees for 40 minutes. Let stand in oven with heat off about 15 minutes before serving. Entire dish can be prepared in electric fry pan. More water may be added if too thick.

Jane (Mrs. Alan) Forbes, Buffalo, New York

Jane Forbes enjoys teaching Bible classes in neighborhood homes. For twenty-five years she has planned and arranged music for husband Alan Forbes' Youthtime Rallies in Buffalo.

Zucchini Surprise

Charlotte writes: "Zucchini Surprise, a tossed vegetable salad with a sweet and sour dressing, rolls and butter, and fresh fruit for dessert make a satisfying, wholesome dinner for eight."

1 small onion, chopped	2 cans Contadina baby
Butter	tomato slices
2 lbs. ground round steak	1 cup shredded cheese
2 cups sliced zucchini squash	

Sauté onion in butter until tender and remove from pan. Brown meat and remove from pan. Steam gently sliced zucchini squash in pan, removing while still firm.

Toss lightly meat, onion, zucchini, and tomato slices. Heat through, but do not boil. Sprinkle with cheese, and serve when cheese is melted. (Could be put in warm oven for a few minutes until cheese melts.)

Charlotte (Mrs. John) Snowberger, Phoenix, Arizona

Charlotte Snowberger is the wife of a prominent attorney, mother of six children, and is active in church, civic, and community affairs. She also serves on the board of directors of Camelback Girls' Residence. It is always a delight to visit with them in their lovely home in sunny Phoenix.

Stuffed Peppers

1½ lbs. ground beef and pork	6 green peppers
3 tablespoons rice, uncooked	1 10¾-oz. can condensed
2 eggs, beaten	tomato soup
½ teaspoon salt	

Mix meat, rice, eggs, and salt. Cut tops off the peppers and soak in hot water for a couple of minutes. Scoop out seeds and fill with the meat mixture. Stand peppers in casserole or baking pan. Pour tomato soup over them and bake in a slow oven, 300 degrees, for 1 hour.

Anna Myrl (Mrs. Stan) Long, Upland, California

Stan Long manages two Christian Light bookstores, one in Upland and one in Redlands, California. His wife works side by side with him as secretary and bookkeeper and enjoys singing in the choir at their church.

See Anna Myrl Long's other recipe, Potato Casserole, on page 89.

MOCK TACO HOT DISH

1 small onion, chopped	4 tablespoons vinegar
1½ lbs. ground beef	2 tablespoons oil
1 can chili with beans	2 tablespoons sugar
¼ cup water	Salt and pepper to taste
1 onion	Taco chips
1 green pepper	Cheddar cheese, shredded
1 No. 2 can of tomatoes	Lettuce, shredded

Brown onion and ground beef. Add chili with beans and water. Simmer 30 minutes.

In a blender, or by hand, chop the following ingredients: onion, green pepper, tomatoes, mixing in the vinegar, oil, sugar, and salt and pepper to taste.

Mix the blended sauce with the ground beef mixture and heat. (Commercial taco sauce may be substituted.) Serve mixture over taco chips on individual plates. Top with shredded cheddar cheese and shredded lettuce.

Everything put in separate bowls makes it a fix-it-yourself dish, and these tacos are eaten with a fork! Good for lunch, supper, and late evening get-togethers.

Lavon (Mrs. Ray) Hintz, Minneapolis, Minnesota

Lavon directed the "No Greater Love" dramatic production at Minneapolis Gospel Tabernacle. I was guest soloist on the same evening, and it was wonderful working with this lovely and talented musician. Lavon also enjoys reading and writing music.

CHILI RELLENOS BAKE

Stand back everybody. This looks like a hot one!

1 lb. ground beef
½ cup chopped onion
Salt and pepper to taste
2 4-oz. cans green chilies
1½ cups shredded cheese
1½ cups milk
4 beaten eggs

¼ cup all-purpose flour
½ teaspoon salt
Several dashes from bottle of
  hot sauce
Dash of pepper
Corn chips or tostadas
  (optional)

Brown beef and onions; drain and season. Halve chilies and remove seeds. Place half of chilies in baking dish; sprinkle with cheese; top with meat mixture. Repeat. Top with cheese.

Beat together milk, eggs, flour, salt, hot sauce, and pepper. Pour liquid over all and bake at 350 degrees for 40 or 45 minutes. Cool 5 minutes before serving. If desired, add corn chips or tostadas to the recipe.

Clara (Mrs. John) Vandenburgh, Durango, Colorado

Clara and her husband, John, who is a dentist, are very talented musically and have conducted the Vandenburgh Musicale for sixteen years in Riverside, California. It has been a privilege to have shared in these musicales in the past. Clara states very simply: "Jesus Christ is very real in our lives and we want to share Him with others." The Vandenburghs have just released a new record called "Happy and Nice with a Little Spice."

Beef Mexicana

1 lb. round steak, ground
1/4 cup butter
1/4 cup chopped onion
1/4 cup chopped green pepper
1 10¾-oz. can condensed
   tomato soup
1 cup milk

3 cups medium noodles,
   cooked, drained
2 cups whole kernel corn
1/4 cup chopped ripe olives
1½ cups grated process
   American cheese
Salt and pepper to taste
Parsley (optional)

Brown meat in butter. Add onion and green pepper, and cook until tender. Add soup, milk, noodles, corn, olives, and 1 cup of the cheese. Mix well; season to taste. Pour mixture into a buttered 2-quart casserole. Top with remaining ½ cup cheese. Bake at 350 degrees for 25 to 30 minutes. Garnish with parsley. Serves 8.

Margaret (Mrs. Richard H.) Boldt, Jr., Oak Park, Illinois

Margaret is the wife of Dick Boldt, executive director of Cedar Lake Bible Conference, Cedar Lake, Indiana, where I have sung many times. She assists her husband in his work by being conference hostess, dietitian, and staff organist.

Russian Fluff

My mother used to fix this one when she had three hungry teen-agers to feed and not much time. Why it's called "Russian Fluff" no one seems to know, as the ingredients are decidedly "un-Russian"! Here's an easy, busy-day recipe you can prepare ahead and bake at the last minute.

1 cup chopped onions
1/4 cup shortening
1½ lbs. ground beef
¾ teaspoon salt
1/4 teaspoon pepper

1 can peas or 1 pkg. frozen
   peas, cooked
1 10½-oz. can condensed
   tomato soup
3 cups boiled (quick-cook-
   ing) rice

Sauté onions in shortening for 5 minutes. Add meat and cook 10 minutes longer. Add salt, pepper, peas (including liquid), tomato soup, and boiled rice. Pour mixture into 2-quart greased casserole. Bake uncovered in an oven that has not been preheated, 35 to 45 minutes at 325 degrees.

Gwen Waggoner, Granada Hills, Caifornia

My friend Gwen Waggoner loves this recipe and has made it often. In fact, she insisted that I use it in my casserole book, so I'll just give her the credit!

African Chop Suey Casserole

1 lb. ground beef
1 cup chopped celery
1 cup chopped onion
1 small green pepper, chopped
2 teaspoons soy sauce
1 10½-oz. can condensed chicken with rice soup

1 10½-oz. can condensed cream of mushroom soup
1 chicken bouillon cube in 1 cup water
Bean sprouts (optional)
½ cup raw rice (not instant)
Crushed potato chips or chop suey noodles

Brown meat, celery, onion, and green pepper. Add soy sauce, soups, bouillon, and bean sprouts (optional). Add rice last. Pour into baking dish. Bake at 350 degrees for 1 hour. Stir occasionally. Top with crushed potato chips or chop suey noodles the last half hour of baking.

Esther (Mrs. Ralph) Sutera, Mansfield, Ohio

Ralph and Louis Sutera are identical twins who were in my high school graduation class one or two years ago (!). I'll let you guess which one I actually dated once or twice. They are now very actively engaged in evangelistic crusades in the United States and Canada, and God has blessed their ministry in an unusual way.

PLENTY FOR TWENTY

Diane says, "This is a favorite of the ladies at our church in lovely Boca Raton, Florida."

⅓ cup cooking oil
2½ cups chopped onion
2½ cups chopped green pepper
2 cloves garlic, minced
3 lbs. ground beef
1 tablespoon salt
1 teaspoon freshly ground pepper

2 16-oz. cans tomatoes
3 12-oz. cans whole kernel corn
3 cups sliced, pitted black olives
1½ lbs. medium noodles, cooked and drained
3 cups grated, sharp cheddar cheese

Preheat oven to 350 degrees. Lightly grease two 9 x 13-inch baking dishes. Heat cooking oil and sauté onion, green pepper, and garlic in very large saucepan or Dutch oven. Add ground beef. Continue cooking until browned. Add remaining ingredients except cheese. Pour into baking dishes. Cover and bake for 45 minutes in a 350-degree oven. Top with grated cheese. Bake 15 minutes more.

Diane (Mrs. Vernon) Drake, Boca Raton, Florida

See Diane's other recipes, Pork Chop Casserole on page 32, and Drake's Chicken Delight on page 69.

SHEPHERD'S PIE

4 cups mashed potatoes
1 medium onion, chopped
2 lbs. ground chuck
Worcestershire sauce

Catsup
Salt and pepper
1 egg white
1 tomato

Boil and mash enough potatoes to cover your casserole. Sauté onions and put aside. Brown ground chuck a few minutes in a bit of water. Add Worcestershire sauce, catsup, salt and pepper (few shakes of each). Add onions. Drain off excess grease.

Fill casserole with beef mixture and top with mashed potatoes. Brush potatoes with egg white and bake in 350-degree oven for about 20 minutes. Remove from oven, top with slices of tomato, and broil for 2 to 3 minutes until golden brown. Mmmm! Kids love it.

Nancy (Mrs. Arthur) DeMoss, Villanova, Pennsylvania

Nancy DeMoss says that this recipe originally came from England and is a favorite of all seven of her children. Nancy is an accomplished musician and records for Supreme Records. She gives a great amount of her time to singing and speaking for the Christian Women's Club of America as well as other organizations. With her husband, Arthur DeMoss, president of National Liberty Group, she edits and publishes several widely circulated Christian books.

YUM YUM CASSEROLE

This is really a "quickie" which you can throw together in about 10 minutes. Double it if you have a larger family.

1 lb. ground beef	1 10½-oz. can condensed
1 can chow mein noodles	cream of mushroom soup

Brown meat, and mix with noodles and soup. Bake at 350 degrees for 20–25 minutes.

Elaine (Mrs. Les) Sutter, Morton, Illinois

I met the Sutters on the set of the movie "Beloved Enemy" several years ago. Elaine is a second-grade teacher, and Les is an analyst at Caterpillar Tractor Company. They have one daughter, Victoria.

HONEYMOON GOULASH

1 lb. ground beef
Salt and pepper to taste
Chili pepper and cayenne
   pepper (optional)
1 10¾-oz. can condensed
   tomato soup

1 10½-oz. can condensed
   cream of mushroom soup
½ lb. spaghetti, cooked
Parmesan cheese

Brown ground beef and season with salt and pepper (and chili pepper and cayenne pepper if you like it hot). Add soups and simmer for ½ hour. Mix with cooked spaghetti and serve with Parmesan cheese. For variation, add drained tomatoes, or mushrooms, or peppers, or all three. Put any kind of cheese in it or mix with a little sour cream before serving. Use macaroni or rice instead of spaghetti.

Joan (Mrs. Robert) Nesbit, Collinsville, Illinois

Joanie is a friend from high school days and we have shared a lot of "fun" memories. She is the mother of two boys, has a husband who likes her cooking, and, she claims, has a "neurotic dog." Joanie says that after twenty years, her husband still asks for this Honeymoon Goulash.

PORK CHOP AND LIMA BEAN CASSEROLE

1½ cups cooked dried lima
   beans (canned)
6 center-cut pork chops
1 teaspoon salt
2 tablespoons flour
1½ cups water
⅓ cup catsup

2 tablespoons brown sugar
3 tablespoons minced onion
¾ teaspoon ground mustard
½ teaspoon ground black
   pepper
¼ teaspoon instant garlic
   powder
1 small bay leaf

Turn beans into a 2½-quart covered casserole. Trim fat from chops and save. Rub chops with salt, then sprinkle them with flour and brown on both sides in fat trimmings. Arrange chops over beans. Combine 1½ cups water with remaining ingredients. Pour over meat and beans. Cover and bake in preheated slow oven, 325 degrees, 1½ hours, or until chops are tender. Remove cover and bake 20 minutes more. Serves 6.

Marian (Mrs. Bix) Reichner, Paoli, Pennsylvania

Marian writes that she met her husband, Bix, when she was fourteen in a Methodist Sunday school. (I met my husband when I was twelve and he was the "boy next door"!) Among her other accomplishments, Marian has served on the local school board and has written a column for a newspaper. She also paints portraits and landscapes. Bix Reichner is a talented composer and has a number of well-known songs to his credit. One of his best known in the Christian field is "If You Know the Lord."

Holiday Roast Pork
with Apricot-and-Prune Stuffing

10-12-lb., bone in, fresh ham	½ cup unsifted flour
1 cup pitted dried prunes	2 13¾-oz. cans chicken broth
1 cup dried apricots	6 spiced crab apples
2 teaspoons salt	Parsley sprigs
⅛ teaspoon pepper	

Preheat oven to 325 degrees. Wipe ham with damp paper towels. Trim fat to about ¼-inch thickness, leaving any skin. Score skin into 1-inch diamonds, to make "crackling"; score fat into diamonds. With a long, sharp knife, make deep slits to the bone all over the surface, 2 or 3 inches apart. Using fingers, push prunes and apricots alternately into slits. Rub surface with 2 teaspoons salt and the pepper. Insert meat thermometer into thickest part of meat, being careful to avoid slits.

Place roast, fat side up, on rack in shallow, open roasting pan. Roast in oven, uncovered, 2 hours. Drain off fat, and discard. Pour 1 cup water over roast; roast ½ hour longer. Pour 1 cup water over roast; repeat every half hour until meat thermometer registers 180 degrees. (Total roasting time is approximately 6 hours.) If the roast is getting too brown, place a sheet of foil loosely over top. Remove roast to heated platter; keep warm.

Pour drippings into a 2-cup measuring cup. Let stand a few minutes; skim off fat, and discard. You should have about 1 cup drippings. In small bowl, stir flour and 1 cup chicken broth until smooth and flour is dissolved. In medium saucepan, combine remaining broth and the drippings; heat to boiling. Slowly add flour mixture, stirring constantly until mixture returns to boiling and thickens. Reduce heat; simmer 5 minutes, stirring occasionally. Add salt to taste.

To serve roast: Skewer 3 apples on each of 2 wooden skewers; insert skewers in bone end of ham. Garnish with parsley. Pass gravy. Makes 10 to 12 servings.

SPARERIBS WORCESTERSHIRE

3 lbs. spareribs, cut into serving size pieces	½ cup orange marmalade
6 tablespoons Worcestershire sauce	3 tablespoons finely chopped onion
	1½ teaspoons salt

Brush 3 tablespoons of the Worcestershire sauce over both sides of ribs. Bake on rack in pan in 400-degree oven for 45 minutes, turning occasionally. Pour off drippings. Reduce heat to 350 degrees. Combine remaining Worcestershire sauce with remaining ingredients; mix well. Brush sauce over ribs. Bake 20 to 30 minutes, basting until nicely glazed. Serves 4.

Spareribs with Apples and Squash

4 lbs. spareribs, cut into 2-rib portions
1 tablespoon salt
½ teaspoon pepper
½ cup minced onion
2 tablespoons butter or margarine
3 cups apple juice
½ cup cider vinegar
3 tablespoons brown sugar
1½ teaspoons cinnamon
1 teaspoon salt
2 tablespoons cornstarch
2 acorn squash
4 baking apples

Sprinkle spareribs with 1 tablespoon salt and ½ teaspoon pepper; arrange, meaty side up, in a shallow roasting pan. Bake at 400 degrees for 30 minutes. Drain off fat.

Sauté onion in butter; stir in 2¾ cups apple juice, vinegar, brown sugar, cinnamon, and 1 teaspoon salt. Heat to boiling. Blend cornstarch with remaining ¼ cup apple juice; gradually add to hot mixture. Cook, stirring constantly, until thickened and clear. Spoon apple juice mixture over spareribs. Cover pan with foil; bake at 350 degrees for 1 hour.

Cut each squash into 8 sections. Core apples; cut in half crosswise. Arrange squash and apples around ribs; spoon sauce over all. Cover and bake about 1 hour longer, or until spareribs and squash are cooked. Serves 8.

Pork Chop Casserole

2-2½ lbs. pork chops
1 medium onion, chopped
1 tablespoon vinegar
1 tablespoon brown sugar
½ cup diced celery
½ cup Worcestershire sauce
1 tablespoon mustard
1 8-oz. can tomato sauce
½ cup water

Brown pork chops. Remove from pan and sauté onion until brown. Add rest of ingredients to pan and heat for 5 minutes. Lay pork chops in casserole and pour hot mixture over the meat. Bake in 350-degree oven for one hour. Then reduce heat to 300 degrees and bake 15 minutes more. Serves 4–5.

Diane (Mrs. Vernon) Drake, Boca Raton, Florida

Did you ever think what fun it might be to be a triplet? Diane could tell us a little about that! She and her two sisters sang as "The Mackinson Triplet Trio" as they were growing up in northern New Jersey. All three girls became registered nurses, and all are now married and have lovely families. Since we're already thinking in "threes," I decided to share three of Diane's recipes with you (one for each sister).

See Diane's other recipes, Plenty for Twenty on page 27 and Drake's Chicken Delight on page 69.

SWEET AND SOUR PORK

1¼ lbs. pork, cut in 1-inch cubes
1 teaspoon salt
⅛ teaspoon pepper
¼ cup shortening
½ can pineapple chunks (1 lb., 41½ oz. size) (Drain, reserve syrup)

1 green pepper, cut in strips
¼ cup cornstarch
⅔ cup sugar
2 cups chicken bouillon
⅔ cup vinegar
⅛ cup soy sauce
Hot cooked rice

Season pork with salt and pepper. Place shortening and pork in 13 x 9 x 2-inch metal baking pan. Bake at 400 degrees for 1 hour to brown meat, stirring often. Spoon off fat. Add pineapple and green pepper to meat.

In Dutch oven, combine cornstarch and sugar; stir in bouillon, vinegar, soy sauce, and reserved pineapple syrup. Cook and stir until mixture thickens and bubbles. Pour into pan and combine with meat. Continue baking at 400 degrees for 45 minutes. Stir occasionally. Serve over hot cooked rice. Serves 6.

Doris (Mrs. Lloyd) Sutherland, Grand Rapids, Michigan

I am enjoying being hostess of a children's weekly television program called "Treehouse Club," sponsored by Child Evan-

gelism Fellowship and seen nationally. Lloyd Sutherland is the executive producer of the show, and his wife, Doris, is his "Right-Hand Gal."

SWEET POTATO SURPRISE

Here's a sweet potato recipe with a little "zing"!

4 medium sweet potatoes
1 tablespoon butter
Dash of black pepper, salt, and nutmeg to taste
4 cups cooked ham, cut into 1-inch cubes
Shortening
1 green pepper, cut into ringed slices
2 cups pineapple chunks, drained

1 cup sweet pickles, sliced or chunked
2 medium tomatoes, cut in wedges
1 small jar pimentos, drained
½ cup water
3 tablespoons cornstarch
3 tablespoons vinegar
2 teaspoons sugar
1 tablespoon molasses
1 cup chicken bouillon
Dots of butter

Boil sweet potatoes until done. Drain thoroughly. Add 1 tablespoon of butter, dash of black pepper, salt, and nutmeg. Whip and set aside.

Lightly brown the ham cubes in a skillet with small amount of shortening. Add pepper slices, pineapple chunks, pickles, tomatoes, pimentos and water. Simmer for five minutes.

Make a sauce by combining the cornstarch, vinegar, sugar, molasses, and chicken bouillon. Heat, stirring constantly until thickened and clear (about 2 minutes).

Pour sauce over ham mixture and stir gently. Pour into baking dish. Top with whipped sweet potatoes. Dot with butter. Bake for 30 minutes in 375-degree oven. Serve hot from oven.

Ida L. (Mrs. Roland) Gerdes, Grand Rapids, Michigan

Ida Gerdes is the mother of two, and the wife of Roland Gerdes, executive director of Child Evangelism Fellowship. Mrs. Gerdes says that she enjoys sharing the work that her husband represents.

HAM AND NOODLES

Wonder what to do with leftover ham? Here's one good idea and your husband won't know you're serving leftovers . . .

1 cup uncooked noodles	½ teaspoon pepper
4 tablespoons butter	½ cup chopped green pepper
2 beaten eggs	1 tablespoon grated onion
1 cup milk	1 cup buttered bread crumbs
1½ cups chopped, cooked ham	

Measure cup of noodles cut in short lengths. Cook in boiling water and drain when done. To noodles add butter, beaten eggs, milk, ham, and seasonings, including green pepper and onion. Place in greased baking dish. Top with buttered crumbs. Cover and bake 40 minutes in 350-degree oven. (One cup of mushrooms may be added. Beef or chicken may be used instead of ham.)

Miriam (Mrs. Lloyd) Knight, Mississauga, Ontario, Canada

Miriam Knight says she became a Christian in her mid-teens, is married to a "terrific guy" (She is! Singer and recording artist Lloyd Knight), and divides her time between her three children, her part-time job as a secretary, and her Sunday school teaching.

CANADIAN BACON AND POTATO PIE

2 cups sliced peeled potato	½ lb. sliced Canadian bacon
2 cups sliced peeled apples	¼ cup water
1 cup sliced onion	1 stick piecrust mix
2 teaspoons salt	Cream or 1 slightly beaten
¼ teaspoon pepper	egg white

Layer half of first 3 ingredients in 2½-quart casserole, seasoning with salt and pepper. Add a layer of bacon. Repeat layers, ending with bacon. Pour in ¼ cup water.

Prepare piecrust mix as directed on package; roll out and adjust on top of casserole. Cut several slits in crust to allow steam to escape. Bake in moderate oven, 375 degrees, 1 hour, or until golden. Brush with cream or egg white 15 minutes before pie is done. Serves 6.

CALIFORNIA CASSEROLE

2 lbs. veal round steak	1¾ cups small cooked onions
⅓ cup flour	(1-lb. can, drained)
1 teaspoon paprika	1 10½-oz. can condensed
¼ cup vegetable shortening	cream of chicken soup
	1 can water (part onion
	liquid)

Coat steak with mixture of flour and paprika. Pound mixture into meat; cut into 2-inch cubes. Brown meat thoroughly in shortening. Transfer to 14 x 10 x 2-inch baking dish or 3-quart casserole (or 2 smaller baking dishes). Add onions.

Heat soup in skillet used for browning, blending in water (part onion liquid may be used). Bring to a boil and pour over meat. Bake uncovered in moderate oven, 350 degrees, about 45 minutes until meat is tender. Top with 14 to 16 butter crumb dumplings.

Increase oven temperature to 425 degrees; bake uncovered for 20 to 25 minutes until deep golden brown. Serve with sauce.

Butter crumb dumplings:

2⅛ cups sifted flour
4 teaspoons baking powder
½ teaspoon salt
1 teaspoon poultry seasoning
1 teaspoon celery seed
1 teaspoon onion flakes

1 tablespoon poppy seed (optional)
¼ cup salad oil
1 cup milk
¼ cup melted butter
1 cup bread crumbs

Sift dry ingredients together into mixing bowl. Add salad oil and milk, stirring just until moistened. Drop rounded tablespoonfuls of dough into a mixture of melted butter and bread crumbs. Roll to coat with crumbs.

Sauce:

1 10½-oz. can condensed cream of chicken soup

1 cup sour cream

Combine soup with sour cream. Heat just to boiling.

MOROCCAN LAMB CASSEROLE

Marjory says this is a recipe which she learned from her sister who was a missionary in Morocco.

1 onion, chopped
Cooking oil or butter
1 teaspoon cinnamon
1 lb. stewing lamb, cut in pieces
Water

1 teaspoon turmeric
Salt to taste
Potatoes, peeled and cut up
Black olives
1 tablespoon lemon juice

Sauté onion in oil or butter. Sprinkle on cinnamon while frying. Add lamb slowly, stirring to keep from sticking. Place in casserole and cover with water. Add turmeric and salt to taste. Put in potatoes and olives (as many as you like!). Cook for 2 hours at 350 degrees. Ten minutes before serving add lemon juice. Serve with warm, fresh bread.

Marjory (Mrs. Paul) Owens, Chateau d'Oex, Switzerland

Marjory Owens describes herself in the following words: "Wife of hotel manager, former music teacher, mother of charmer, and loves cooking when time." All these things are true; however, Marjory is much too modest. She is a very talented musician who sings and plays the piano beautifully. I was thrilled to hear Marjory and her husband, Paul, sing one Sunday evening in the Rosat Hotel (which her husband manages) in Chateau d'Oex, Switzerland.

FRANKFURTER AND POTATO CASSEROLE

Betty Cooper writes: "This was an original concoction from back in 'very tight budget' days! It's still a family favorite."

5 or 6 medium potatoes	2 cups milk
1 lb. frankfurters	½ lb. Velveeta cheese
3 tablespoons margarine	Seasoned pepper
4 tablespoons flour	Paprika

Dice and cook potatoes until done, but not too soft. Drain. Combine with thinly sliced frankfurters. Make sauce of other ingredients and turn all into a casserole. Sprinkle with seasoned pepper and paprika and bake at 325 degrees for about half an hour, or until nicely browned.

Betty (Mrs. Ed) Cooper, Altoona, Pennsylvania

"Pastor Ed" and wife Betty enjoy their pastorate at the First Baptist Church, Altoona, Pennsylvania. Ed also has a radio ministry called "Mid-Day Harmony," which is aired on several stations.

Bratwurst and Fried Peppered Cabbage

1 medium size head white cabbage	2 tablespoons sour cream
¼ cup butter	6 bratwursts
Salt and freshly ground black pepper	Flour
	½ cup dehydrated onions

Wash cabbage, remove core, and grate into fine pieces. Melt butter in a large frying pan over medium heat. (Careful! Don't burn the butter.) Add cabbage and sauté, turning constantly for about 1½ to 2 minutes, just until cabbage is heated through, but not wilted. (Do not overcook.) Season with salt and very heavy pepper to taste. Stir in sour cream.

If bratwurst is preblanched, place in hot water, not boiling, until they are heated through. Dust in flour and place in frying pan over medium heat. Brown slowly on both sides, then place on or beside the peppered cabbage. Reconstitute onions according to package instructions, and sauté until nicely browned and crisp. Sprinkle over sausage before serving.

Gloria Roe (Mrs. Ron) Robertson, Rolling Hills, California

How's that for a good hearty German dish? Gloria Roe took time out of her heavy schedule as mother of three, composer, and recording artist to share this one with us. Gloria is married to busy attorney, Ron Robertson.

Frank 'n' Noodle Barbecue

1 lb. frankfurters	1 cup chili sauce
¼ cup salad oil	2 tablespoons brown sugar
¼ cup finely chopped onion	¼ cup lemon juice
½ teaspoon salt	3½ cups cooked noodles
1 tablespoon Worcestershire sauce	Barbecue sauce

Combine frankfurters, salad oil, onion, salt, Worcestershire sauce, chili sauce, brown sugar, and lemon juice in a saucepan and simmer for 15 minutes. Place 3½ cups cooked noodles in bottom of 2½-quart baking dish. Arrange franks on top and pour barbecue sauce over all. Bake in a moderate oven, 350 degrees, for 30 minutes. Makes 4 to 6 servings.

Hot Dogs and Kraut

Stuffing:

1 medium onion, finely chopped
1 tablespoon butter

1 cup Pepperidge Farm bread stuffing

Sauté onion in butter until golden brown. Add to stuffing.

1 large can sauerkraut (add a little water)
½ apple, finely diced
1 tablespoon caraway seed

⅓ cup pickle relish, drained
8 frankfurters
8 slices bacon, partially cooked

Mix the kraut, apple, caraway seed, and drained pickle relish together and pour into greased casserole.

Slit 8 frankfurters partially and stuff with stuffing mixture. Wrap partially cooked bacon around frankfurters. Lay on top of sauerkraut mixture in casserole and bake at 400 degrees for 20 minutes.

Florence (Mrs. Harry) Bristow, Glenside, Pennsylvania

Harry and Florence Bristow have been my friends for several years, dating back to the time when we lived in Pennsylvania. Harry is founder and director of Christian Cinema, Inc., a film ministry and bookstore near Philadelphia, Pennsylvania. He is also a radio and television personality in the Philadelphia area and is responsible for awarding "Oscars" to those in the Christian field for outstanding performance. His capable wife, Florence, is one of those people who "wears well." She leads a busy and active life as Harry's "right hand gal."

Shellfish and Fish

There is a love that feeds
On others' wants and needs
And gives to the one who
    fills them.
A love so devouring it
    cannot live
Without its object,
Nor let it go.
It is a heavy love.
It is a selfish, give-me, tightfisted parasite

There is a love that is strong enough
To set its object free
And wish it well
In its endeavors,
A love that lives in light
    and freedom.
It gives its best, asks no thing and is openhanded.

How can love change?
Because there is another Love,
One who loves still more,
And He has changed my love from
    the first to
    the second.

Which love is yours?

Lois Fiedler

Baked Clams from Blue Point

2 tablespoons olive oil
2 tablespoons onion, minced
2 cloves garlic, minced
1 large can minced clams, drained
½ of liquid from drained clams

¼ cup Italian seasoned bread crumbs
2 tablespoons Parmesan cheese
2 tablespoons bread crumbs

Sauté onion and garlic in oil. Add drained clams plus half of liquid. Mix with ¼ cup bread crumbs. Place in clam shells and sprinkle with cheese and 2 tablespoons bread crumbs. Bake at 350 degrees for 25 minutes.

Lobster Thermidor

3 pkgs. (8 oz. each) frozen rock lobster tails (12 2-oz. tails), or 6 lobster tails (5 to 6 oz. each)
1 tablespoon whole pickling spice
2 shallots or 4 green onions, minced
½ cup butter
6 tablespoons flour

1 teaspoon each: salt, dry mustard
½ teaspoon each: tarragon, chervil
⅛ teaspoon white pepper
2 cups half and half
½ cup grated Parmesan cheese
Melted butter
Parsley sprigs, garnish

Parboil small frozen lobster tails by dropping into boiling salted water to which pickling spice has been added. When water reboils, drain immediately; drench with cold water. (For 5 to 6-ounce tails, simmer for 6 to 7 minutes or 1 minute per ounce plus 1 for pot.) Cut away underside membrane. Remove meat; cut into ½-inch slices. Reserve shells.

Sauté shallots in ½ cup butter; stir in flour and seasonings. Gradually add half and half. Cook, stirring constantly, until thickened. Boil 1 minute. Add 3 tablespoons cheese. Fold in lobster; heat. Spoon into shells; top with remaining cheese and melted butter. Broil until golden. Garnish with parsley. Serves 6.

CRABMEAT CHANTILLY

Turn off your calorie counter for this one. (You can go back on your diet tomorrow!)

1 lb. lump crabmeat	Salt and pepper to taste
2 tablespoons butter	2 pkgs. frozen asparagus
2 tablespoons flour	1 cup whipped cream
2¼ cups light cream	4 tablespoons Parmesan cheese

Sauté the crabmeat lightly in the butter. Add the flour and cream (you may substitute cream of mushroom or celery soup for cream if you wish); season and cook until thickened, fork-stirring to keep the crabmeat in lumps. Cook the asparagus and drain. Place asparagus in the bottom of a well-buttered casserole. Pour the crabmeat mixture over asparagus, spread the whipped cream over crabmeat mixture, and sprinkle with the cheese and brown under broiler.

Note: Substitute any seafood or chicken for the crabmeat and add any appropriate vegetable in place of the asparagus. For a nice change, add slices of avocado, mushrooms, or browned almonds before spreading the whipped cream. Serves 4 to 6 people.

Karen (Mrs. Don) Wyrtzen, Grand Rapids, Michigan

Karen is the pretty wife of pianist-composer Don Wyrtzen and the daughter-in-law of Word of Life's Jack Wyrtzen. Karen enjoys creative cooking, needlework, reading, and her tennis lessons. Don is with Zondervan Publishing House of Grand Rapids, Michigan, and he and Karen have two children.

EASY CRABMEAT CASSEROLE

Here's a fast dish for a day when you want to impress someone with your gourmet cooking skills and don't have all day to spend in the kitchen. Shirley penned these words above the recipe: "Delicious! Unique! Tasty! Easy! Expensive!" Watch out for that last one.

1 cup elbow macaroni
2 cans cream of shrimp
  soup
2 pkgs. frozen macaroni and
  cheese

2 pkgs. frozen crabmeat (1
  pkg. will do)
Buttered bread crumbs

Cook 1 cup macaroni and add to the other ingredients. Mix well and place in baking dish. Top with buttered bread crumbs. Bake 1 hour at 350 degrees. Serves 8.

Shirley (Mrs. Frederik) Jacobsen, Huntington, Connecticut

Shirley Jacobsen is church secretary for Pastor Andersen at one of my favorite churches, Evangelical Free of Trumble, Connecticut.

BROCCOLI-CRABMEAT CASSEROLE

"Evie" McNutt says this recipe "kind of fits in with the 'fish concept' for which New England is known."

2 boxes frozen broccoli,
  thawed
1 can crabmeat
1 10½-oz. can condensed
  cream of celery soup

¼ large bag Pepperidge Farm
  stuffing mix
Grated Parmesan cheese or
  cheddar cheese

Spread broccoli in buttered casserole. Put crabmeat over

broccoli and ½ can celery soup. Spread layer of stuffing mixed with water to moisten. Add other half can of celery soup. Sprinkle grated cheese on top. Bake at 350 degrees for 30 minutes. Serve with baked rice and green salad.

Evelyn (Mrs. Tal) McNutt, Danvers, Massachusetts

Evie is food supervisor for their four camps at Rumney Bible Conference in New Hampshire and is cook for Winter Snow Camp. She enjoys being in full-time Christian camping ministry. Her husband, Tal, is general director of the New England Fellowship of Evangelicals, which includes ministries in various areas such as camps, crusades, and youth rallies.

OYSTER-CORN CASSEROLE

Club-style crackers
1 large can yellow cream-style corn
1 large can oysters, drained
1 small can oysters (reserve liquid for egg-milk mixture)

Butter
3 eggs
Milk (see procedure)
Salt and pepper
Paprika

Butter *shallow* casserole. Line bottom with layer of crushed crackers. Alternate layers of corn, oysters, and cracker crumbs. Add dots of butter generously to corn layers.

Beat eggs in large measuring bowl or pitcher. Add liquid from small can oysters. Then add enough milk to bring total liquid measurement up to 3 cups. Sprinkle with salt and pepper.

Pour liquid over corn-oyster mixture. With a knife, make several small holes for liquid to run down into layers. Sprinkle with paprika, and bake 45 minutes in 375-degree oven. (Mary says if it's not "good and brown," turn oven up to 400 degrees and brown for a few more minutes.) This can be precooked for 30 to 40 minutes and heated through *thoroughly* just before serving.

Mary (Mrs. Dave) Crowley, Dallas, Texas

"Warm" and "generous" are two words which best describe Mary Crowley. (Anyone who says she cooks with "love and butter" is definitely my kind of gal!) Mary's shop, Home Interiors and Gifts, on Regal Row in Dallas, is the kind of place you could happily spend a week just sightseeing! Despite her demanding schedule as a business woman, Mary is actively engaged in many church and civic projects.

OYSTER-MUSHROOM PIE

1 lb. mushrooms
8 tablespoons butter or margarine
1 small onion, grated
3 tablespoons flour
Salt, pepper, nutmeg, and cayenne

1½ cups heavy cream
2½ dozen oysters
Rich pastry
1 egg, beaten

Remove caps from mushrooms and reserve. Chop stems very fine and cook in 4 tablespoons butter 2 to 3 minutes. Grate onion into mushrooms and cook, stirring occasionally, until most of liquid is evaporated. Stir in flour and add seasonings to taste. Gradually add cream and cook, stirring, until smooth and thickened.

Sauté mushroom caps in remaining butter until just cooked. Put caps and oysters in 2-quart casserole and pour sauce over top. Put a cup or other support in center of casserole. Roll pastry to fit top and adjust on mixture. If desired, decorate with small pastry designs. Brush with egg and bake in very hot oven, 450 degrees, for 10 minutes, or until browned. Makes 6 servings.

BOB'S SCALLOPED OYSTERS

20 or more oyster crackers
¾ cup (1½ sticks) butter or
  margarine
1 pint fresh oysters or 1 large
  can oysters

1 teaspoon Worcestershire
  sauce
½ teaspoon salt
½ teaspoon pepper
2 cups milk

Alternate layers of crackers, butter, and oysters in buttered casserole. Sprinkle portion of Worcestershire sauce on each layer and salt and pepper to taste. End with crackers on top. Cover with milk until it can be seen at top. Bake at 300 degrees for 45 minutes, or until brown. Serves 8.

Betty (Mrs. Bob) Baggott, Opelika, Alabama

I met Betty for the first time when we stayed at the same hotel in Switzerland, and we "clicked" immediately. Besides being the wife of a minister, Betty is the mother of three, a free-lance writer, and also does some singing. (Aside from Flo: She is also one of the most naturally funny people I know, and is a delight to be around!)

CRAB AND SHRIMP CASSEROLE

1 medium green pepper,
  chopped
1 medium onion, chopped
1 cup celery, chopped
1 6½-ounce can crabmeat,
  flaked
1 4½-ounce can shrimp,
  cleaned and flaked

½ teaspoon salt
⅛ teaspoon pepper
1 teaspoon Worcestershire
  sauce
1 cup mayonnaise
1 cup buttered bread crumbs

Heat oven to 350 degrees. Mix all ingredients except bread

crumbs and place in greased 1-quart baking dish. Sprinkle with crumbs and bake 30 minutes. 6 to 8 servings.

Diane (Mrs. Ron) Susek, Washington, D.C.

Lovely singer and recording artist Diane Susek sends this yummy casserole. Diane recently graduated from Peabody Conservatory, records with Heartwarming and Impact Records, and travels full time with her husband, Evangelist Ron Susek, in evangelistic work. Diane claims she is a novice cook, but says it's almost impossible to fail with this one.

BAKED STUFFED SHRIMP

1 lb. fresh large shrimp, in shells
1 6-oz. pkg. frozen king crab, thawed, drained
¾ cup coarse fresh bread crumbs
½ cup butter, melted

1 tablespoon minced parsley
½ teaspoon salt
⅛ teaspoon garlic powder
Paprika
Grated Parmesan cheese

Shell and devein raw shrimp; wash. Slit along vein side as deep as possible. Finely chop crab meat; mix with bread crumbs, ⅓ of butter, parsley, salt, and garlic powder. Press filling in each shrimp; place in a shallow buttered baking dish. Sprinkle any remaining filling between shrimp. Top shrimp with a little paprika and cheese. Bake at 350 degrees for 20 minutes, basting with remaining butter. Serves 4.
Note: About 12 ounces large frozen shelled shrimp may be substituted for fresh shrimp in shells. Thaw before stuffing. Dish serves about 6 as an appetizer.

SHRIMP TETRAZZINI

½ lb. uncooked spaghetti
½ lb. mushrooms, sliced
2 tablespoons butter
½ lb. cooked shrimp, cleaned and split lengthwise

2 10½-oz. cans condensed cream of mushroom soup
½ cup light cream
⅓ cup Parmesan cheese, grated

Heat oven to 375 degrees. Cook spaghetti in boiling water. Drain. Sauté mushrooms in butter 2 to 3 minutes. In 2-quart casserole, layer spaghetti, mushrooms, and shrimp. Combine soup and cream. Pour over shrimp mixture; sprinkle with cheese. Bake 25 minutes or until hot. If necessary, place under broiler for a few minutes to brown cheese. Makes 6 servings.

Janice (Mrs. Ralph) Franzen, Wheaton, Illinois

Janice Gosnell Franzen is Women's Editor and columnist for one of my favorite publications, Christian Life *magazine. We are indebted to Jan for this luscious shrimp dish.*

FRENCH FRIED RICE WITH SHRIMP

1 cup chopped green pepper
1 cup chopped celery
¾ cup chopped onion
1 small garlic clove, chopped
5 tablespoons margarine
1 small can mushrooms, drained

1 lb. cooked shrimp
4 cups cold cooked Minute Rice
4 tablespoons soy sauce
2 tablespoons chopped pimento (optional)

Sauté green pepper, celery, onion, and garlic in margarine for 5 minutes. Add rest of ingredients and heat thoroughly in large frying pan. Serve with extra soy sauce.

Helen (Mrs. Paul) Stewart, Grand Rapids, Michigan

Paul Stewart is director of promotion and public relations for Child Evangelism Fellowship. His wife, Helen, enjoys first of all being a wife, mother, and homemaker. Other pleasures and interests include being a Good News teacher for sixteen years, a local CEF director for eight years, and being a member of the choir at Calvary Church in Grand Rapids.

CASSEROLE OF SEAFOOD

From the land of swaying palms and fragrant sea breezes comes this mouth-watering seafood casserole sent to us by Velma Loveless.

3 hard-cooked eggs, sliced	1 cup American cheese, diced
1 cup tuna fish	Salt to taste
⅔ cup shrimp, cooked	White sauce
1 cup crabmeat, cooked	1 cup dry bread crumbs
1 cup canned mushrooms, drained	¼ cup butter, melted

Arrange eggs in bottom of buttered casserole. Cover with tuna, shrimp, and crabmeat. Add mushrooms, cheese, and salt to taste.

Pour white sauce, recipe below, over contents of casserole. Mix bread crumbs and butter and sprinkle over top. Bake in a moderate oven, 350 degrees, 35 minutes.

White sauce:	2 cups milk
4 tablespoons butter	1 teaspoon salt
4 tablespoons flour	Pepper to taste

Make white sauce by melting butter, stirring in flour. Add milk gradually; then add 1 teaspoon salt and pepper to taste. Cook over low heat, stirring constantly until thickened.

Velma (Mrs. Wendell P.) Loveless, Honolulu, Hawaii

Wendell P. Loveless is a name well known and loved in the Christian field. Did you know that he was the very first director of Moody Bible Institute's radio station, WMBI? He was on the faculty and staff at Moody for twenty-two years and was featured on daily broadcasts there. Now he is pastor of the

First Chinese Church in Honolulu and also broadcasts daily on two radio stations. I remember him fondly for a lovely record review he wrote in Moody Monthly *for a brand new recording artist (me!) thirteen years ago. His wife, Velma, works at his side (which is a full-time job) and enjoys reading as a hobby.*

FRUITS-OF-THE-SEA CASSEROLE

1 16-oz. package frozen flounder or cod fillets, thawed
1 lb. shelled and deveined shrimp
2 8-oz. cans minced clams
1½ 16-oz. packages small shell macaroni
1½ cups butter or margarine
1 large bunch celery, cut in ½-inch slices (about 5 cups)

1½ cups all-purpose flour
4 cups milk
1 bunch green onions, cut in 1-inch pieces
3 chicken bouillon cubes or envelopes
5 teaspoons salt
¼ teaspoon pepper

About 2 hours before serving:

With knife, cut fillets into serving pieces; drain fillets and shrimp on paper towels. In strainer, over 4-cup measure or large bowl, drain clams; add enough water to clam liquid to measure 4 cups. Prepare macaroni as label directs; drain well. Set these ingredients aside. Preheat oven to 350 degrees.

In 8-quart cook-and-serve Dutch oven* over medium-high heat, in hot butter or margarine, cook celery until tender, about 10 minutes, stirring occasionally. With large spoon, stir flour into celery mixture until well blended. Gradually stir in clam liquid, milk, onions, bouillon cubes, salt and pepper; cook, stirring constantly, until mixture is thickened, about 15 minutes. Gently stir in cooked macaroni, fillets, shrimp and minced clams. Cover and bake 35 minutes or until shrimp are tender when tested with a fork. Serve hot. Makes 12 servings.

*Or, prepare recipe as above in a large kettle but spoon mix-

ture into two greased 3-quart casseroles; cover and bake 25
minutes or until shrimp are tender when tested with a fork.

SEAFOOD MEDLEY

*I can almost smell this one cooking. I sometimes wonder if
I'm not part "fish," the way I love the ocean and seafood. This
has so many "goodies" in it: scallops, crab, shrimp, and
Gruyère cheese. Read on!*

Scallops:
1 lb. scallops
1 cup water
1 small onion, sliced

1 tablespoon parsley, snipped,
 or parsley flakes
2 teaspoons lemon juice
½ teaspoon salt

Combine above ingredients and bring to boil. Simmer 5
minutes. Drain, reserving 1 cup liquid.

White sauce:
4 tablespoons butter or margarine
6 tablespoons flour
1 cup light cream

Reserved scallop liquid
2 oz. Gruyère cheese, cut up
¼ teaspoon pepper

In a saucepan, melt butter. Stir in flour. Add cream and scallop liquid all at once. Over medium heat, cook until mixture
thickens and bubbles, stirring constantly. Remove from heat.
Stir cheese and pepper into white sauce until cheese melts.

Seafood medley:
Scallops, prepared above
8 oz. crab meat, cooked and
 flaked
4 oz. shrimp, boiled

3-oz. can sliced mushrooms,
 drained
1½ cups soft bread crumbs
 (2 slices)
1 tablespoon melted butter

Combine seafoods and mushrooms with the white sauce. Spoon into a 2-quart casserole or 6 individual casseroles. Top with bread crumbs that have been combined with the melted butter. Bake in a 350-degree oven for 30 minutes. 6 servings.

Roselyn (Mrs. Ralph) Norwood, Charlotte, North Carolina

Roselyn is as pretty as her name, and is married to Ralph Norwood, pastor of Calvary Presbyterian Church in Charlotte, North Carolina. She is the mother of two, and recently completed her Master's Degree in Home Economics Education. Ralph is an old buddy from Bob Jones Academy days (one or two years ago!). We met recently at a Bible conference in the East, and had great fun laughing over old times.

HALIBUT IN SOUR CREAM

4 fillets of halibut
2 tablespoons flour
2 tablespoons melted butter
1 pint sour cream

2 tablespoons Worcestershire sauce
1 green pepper, sliced
1 onion, sliced
Lemon and parsley (garnish)

Place fillets in buttered baking dish. Mix together flour and melted butter. Add sour cream and Worcestershire sauce and spread over fillets. Top with green peppers and onions, sliced wafer thin. Butter waxed paper and cover baking dish. Bake in 425-degree oven for 30 minutes. (Remove waxed paper after 10 minutes.) Garnish with lemon and parsley before serving.

Lois (Mrs. Fred) Bock, Tarzana, California

Lois enjoys sewing, homemaking, and doing things with her children. Her husband, arranger-composer Fred Bock, is head of Gentry Publications and is also minister of music at Bel Air Presbyterian Church.

SALMON PIE

1 cup cottage cheese	About 7 oz. salmon
2 tablespoons chopped chives	1 teaspoon salt
1 tablespoon flour	¼ teaspoon white pepper
1 egg, beaten	1 9-inch pie crust
⅓ cup milk	

Mix all ingredients and pour into shell. Bake at 400 degrees for about 30 minutes or until center is firm. Serves 6, or 4 generously.

Note from Mary Lou: Tuna, shrimp, or lobster could easily replace the salmon. Buy the ready-made pie crusts and store in your freezer if you want to "cut corners."

Mary Lou (Mrs. Joe) Bayly, Bartlett, Illinois

Mary Lou's letter to me began, "I just rediscovered your letter in a stack of mail (Joe's comment, 'In a stack of mail going back twelve years!') . . ." I wrote back to Mary Lou and said, "I know the feeling." I have a friend who says she makes such a mess when she cooks that she is in constant fear of being "raided by the health department." I sometimes feel that way about my desk! Mary Lou's husband, Joe, is one of my very favorite poets and authors. His Psalms of My Life *and* View from a Hearse *are two of his books that I treasure, and that you shouldn't miss.*

SCALLOPED SALMON

1⅓ cups packaged, seasoned bread dressing	1 10½-oz. can condensed cream of mushroom soup
⅓ cup melted butter or margarine	1 tablespoon instant minced onion
1 1-lb. can salmon	1 tablespoon dried parsley flakes
3 hard-boiled eggs, chopped	

Preheat oven to 400 degrees. Combine bread dressing and butter; set aside ⅓ cup of the mixture. Drain salmon; add enough water to salmon liquid to make ¾ cup. Combine the 1-cup crumb mixture with the salmon, salmon liquid, eggs, soup, onion, and parsley flakes. Place in a greased, shallow 1-quart baking dish and sprinkle with reserved crumbs. Bake 20 minutes. Serves 4 to 6.

Marvella (Mrs. Ralph) Carmichael, Woodland Hills, California

My sister-in-law Mar Carmichael is making her comeback with this great salmon casserole. (She says she doesn't know how she got in Coffee-time Desserts with a recipe for a chip dip! Come to think of it, I don't either . . .) Mar is the capable wife of composer-conductor Ralph Carmichael, president of Light Records and Lexicon Music. She is not only a wife and mother, but a fantastic cook and interior decorator. Among her many other attributes Mar also comes out with frequent witticisms. When she handed me this recipe she said, "My salmon casserole is very good if you don't like salmon." Translated that means . . . Oh well.

BUFFET FOR TWELVE

How about inviting almost a dozen people over and serving "Buffet for Twelve"?

½ lb. lasagne noodles, broken up (4½ cups)
6 hard-boiled eggs, chopped
2 cans (6 or 7 oz. each) tuna, flaked
1 6-oz. can broiled, sliced mushrooms
½ cup minced onions
½ cup sweet pickle relish
⅓ cup butter or margarine

½ cup flour
2 teaspoons salt (or to taste)
Few drops hot pepper sauce
2 teaspoons Worcestershire sauce
2 tablespoons lemon juice
2 cups chicken broth
2 cups milk or half and half
1 pkg. (twin pack) potato chips, finely crushed

Cook noodles as directed on package. Drain. Combine noodles with next 5 ingredients. In separate pot melt butter; blend next 5 ingredients in butter. Add chicken broth and milk. Stir over low heat until thickened. Add sauce mixture to tuna mixture; toss with fork to blend.

Grease shallow baking dish, about 13 x 9 x 2 inches. Spread thin layer of crushed potato chips in bottom of dish. Spoon in half the tuna mixture; sprinkle with potato chips. Repeat, ending with potato chips. Chill overnight. Bake at 375 degrees for 45 minutes. Makes 12 servings.

Shirley (Mrs. Bruce) Doud, Pekin, Illinois

Shirley Doud is a wife, mother, and a real estate sales consultant. We met several years ago when we worked in the film "Beloved Enemy" together.

Poultry

OH, GOD—
Let me not be a weak broth
   for You,
That slips down the throat
   easily,
But whose taste is nothing,
Whose texture nauseous,
Whose nourishment is nil.
The broth which, when gone,
Leaves You as hungry or more
Than before it came.

Let me be solid food,
That requires chewing,
That must be stabbed with a fork
And cut with a knife.

And, dear God, let me be rare,
So that life's blood is still
   there to see,
Rather than no flavor
   and no texture.

I would be strong for You, Lord.

         Amen.

Lois Fiedler

BAKED CHICKEN SOUFFLE

Margaret Taylor writes that this souffle was served at a wedding breakfast and can be made a day ahead. The recipe can be cut in half for smaller groups. Don't miss trying this one!

9 slices white bread, crust removed
4 cups diced cooked chicken breast (5 chicken breasts)
½ lb. fresh mushrooms, sliced
¼ cup butter
1 can water chestnuts, drained and sliced
½ cup mayonnaise
9 slices process sharp cheese
4 eggs, well beaten

2 cups milk
1 teaspoon salt
1 10½-oz. can cream of mushroom soup
1 10½-oz. can cream of celery soup
1 small jar pimentos, chopped
2 cups buttered coarse bread crumbs

Line a large flat 9 x 13-inch buttered pan with bread. Top with chicken. Sauté mushrooms in butter for 5 minutes. Spoon over chicken with water chestnuts. Dot with mayonnaise. Top with cheese. Combine eggs, milk and salt. Pour over chicken. Mix soups with pimento and spoon over all. Cover with foil and store in refrigerator overnight. Bake at 350 degrees for 1½ hours. Sprinkle bread crumbs over the top for the last 15 minutes. Serves 12–15.

Margaret (Mrs. Kenneth) Taylor, Wheaton, Illinois

I'm sure Margaret's husband, Kenneth Taylor, is well known for many accomplishments, but the most outstanding in my mind is his translation of the Bible into everyday language. In The Living Bible, I Peter 5:7 speaks beautifully and simply: "Let him have all your worries and cares, for he is always thinking about you and watching everything that concerns you."

Poulet de Normandie

Don't you love the sound of "Poulet de Normandie"? It's a recipe with an elegant French name which takes very little American "know-how."

1 pkg. seasoned bread stuffing	½ cup (1 stick) margarine,
1 cup water	melted

Mix above ingredients together lightly. Put half of mixture in a buttered 12 x 8-inch casserole. Set aside rest of mixture.

2½ cups cooked, diced chicken	½ cup chopped celery
½ cup chopped onions	½ cup mayonnaise
¼ cup chopped green onion tops or chives	¾ teaspoon salt

Mix above ingredients thoroughly. Place in casserole over bread mixture. Top with remaining bread mixture.

2 eggs, slightly beaten	1 10½-oz. can condensed
1½ cups milk	cream of mushroom soup
	Grated cheese

Combine eggs and milk and pour evenly over bread mixture. Cover with foil and refrigerate overnight. Take out one hour before baking. Spread mushroom soup over the top. Bake uncovered in 325-degree oven for 40 minutes. Sprinkle with grated cheese. Return to oven for 10 minutes until cheese melts. Serves 8.

Dottie (Mrs. Jim) Groen, Denver, Colorado

Dottie keeps busy with her hobbies of sewing, interior decorating, entertaining, antiquing furniture and being "Mom" to her daughter, Terri. She is also (or should we have said this first!) the wife of active Denver area Youth for Christ director Jim Groen.

Chicken and Rice Casserole

Now here is a chicken and rice casserole to end all chicken and rice casseroles! When is the last time you included pork sausage and bamboo shoots with your chicken and rice? Have hamburgers tomorrow night instead . . . (!)

¾ cup regular rice
¾ cup wild or brown rice
Salt to taste
1 lb. bulk pork sausage
½ cup bamboo shoots
½ cup sliced raw celery
  (slanted slices)
¼-½ cup slivered almonds
½ cup fresh mushrooms or
  1 4-oz. can mushrooms

2 10½-oz. cans condensed
  cream of mushroom soup
1 teaspoon salt
1 teaspoon Worcestershire
  sauce
½ cup water
12 slices chicken (or the
  equivalent)
1½ cups bread crumbs
  (toasted or day old)
¼ cup melted butter or margarine

Cook rice until tender, adding salt. (If wild rice, follow instructions on box.) Drain. While rice is cooking, brown the sausage in a skillet, stirring to break it up. Drain off fat. Stir in bamboo shoots, celery, almonds, mushrooms, soup, salt. Worcestershire sauce, and water. Gently stir this mixture into the cooked, drained rice.

Put half the mixture into a greased baking dish. Arrange chicken on top, then put in rest of rice mixture. Mix the crumbs with butter or margarine and sprinkle over casserole. Bake in a 375-degree oven about 30 minutes. Serves 8–10.

**Catherine Marshall (Mrs. Leonard) LeSourd,
Boynton Beach, Florida**

One of my very favorite writers, Catherine Marshall, has given us such beautiful books as A Man Called Peter, Beyond Ourselves, *and* Christy. *She loves to write and it certainly shows. She also paints, plays the piano, and enjoys making doll clothes for her granddaughter. Catherine Marshall's husband, Leonard LeSourd, is editor of* Guideposts *magazine.*

CASSOULET

This is an authentic French recipe sent to us direct from Montreal by Judy Hornby. Judy says it takes a bit of time, but is well worth the effort and is a special treat for extra special company. It is usually served with a mixed green salad, Roquefort dressing, hot crusty French bread, and ice cream pie as a dessert finale.

1 qt. white beans
¼ lb. lean salt pork
1 bouquet garni (use whatever spices are your favorite)
1 clove of garlic, mashed
1 celery stalk with leaves
2 large onions, chopped
2 small garlic sausages (Italian if available) or 1 lb. regular sausages

1 3½-lb chicken, cut up
Salt and pepper
2 tablespoons bacon drippings
½ cup canned tomato sauce
3 tablespoons parsley (fresh, if available)
1 cup chicken broth
½ lb. cooking ham, diced

Soak beans in water overnight. Drain. Place in a large saucepan with the salt pork, bouquet garni, garlic, celery, and one chopped onion. Cover with water and bring to a boil. Simmer until the beans are tender (about 1½ hours). Add sausages and continue to simmer for 30 minutes longer. Discard bouquet, drain beans, and reserve the liquid.

Meanwhile, season the chicken with salt and pepper and brown in bacon drippings. When nearly crisp, add remaining chopped onion. Finish browning and remove chicken. Add tomato sauce, parsley, and broth to onion in the pan, and simmer 10 minutes.

Cover the bottom of a large cast iron pan or bean pot with the salt pork cut in chunks. Then arrange a layer of beans and sausage, tomato sauce and chicken. Repeat until all ingredients are used, ending with a layer of beans. Pour over enough bean liquid to barely cover and bake covered for 1½ hours at 350 degrees. Remove cover and sprinkle with diced ham. Bake for one additional hour. Serves 8.

Judy (Mrs. Allon) Hornby, Vancouver, British Columbia

I spent a delightful couple of days in Montreal as a guest of the Hornbys after doing a concert in their church. Judy does all her own sewing, upholstering and refinishing furniture and enjoys thoroughly her life as a pastor's wife. Since this book was begun, the Hornbys have moved to Vancouver, British Columbia.

CHICKEN DIVAN

This recipe has an elegant, gourmet look about it, but is really quite simple to make. I once heard Tricia Nixon Cox say that this is one of her father's favorites.

2 10½-oz. cans condensed cream of chicken soup	2 cups sliced cooked chicken
1 cup mayonnaise	½ cup shredded sharp cheese
1 teaspoon lemon juice	½ cup bread crumbs
2 10-oz. pkgs. frozen broccoli spears, cooked	1 tablespoon butter
	Pimento strips

Mix together chicken soup, mayonnaise, and lemon juice. In a casserole, put layers of broccoli, chicken, cheese, and soup mixture. Top with bread crumbs mixed with melted butter. Bake in 350-degree oven for 25 minutes. Garnish with pimento strips.

Dorothy (Mrs. Arthur) Smith, Charlotte, North Carolina

For over thirty years Arthur Smith has entertained audiences with his wholesome, family shows. His very popular television program, "The Arthur Smith Show," is seen throughout the Southeast. Arthur's busy wife, Dorothy, is chairman of the Christian Women's Club of Charlotte. She also serves on the mayor's beautification committee and has won many blue ribbons for flower arranging.

Chicken Spaghetti

Cook stewing hen until meat drops from bone. Last 30 minutes of cooking add 1 bay leaf, several celery leaves, 1 teaspoon salt, pepper. Let cool in broth; then cut into bite-sized cubes.

Sauce:

½ cup (1 stick) butter or margarine
1 medium onion, minced
3 inner stalks celery, finely minced
1 medium green pepper, finely minced
3 tablespoons parsley, minced
1 15-oz. can tomato sauce or 1 6-oz. can tomato paste and 1 can water
1 large can tomatoes, using pulp only
1 tablespoon Worcestershire sauce
½ teaspoon lemon juice
¼ cup sharp cheese, grated
Salt, pepper, wee bit of sugar
2 cups chicken broth
1 large can sliced mushrooms including liquid
1 can sliced ripe olives including liquid
Spaghetti, 1 large package

Heat butter in heavy skillet. Add vegetables and sauté until onion is pale yellow. Add tomato sauce or paste and tomato pulp, Worcestershire sauce, and lemon juice. Add sharp cheese. Salt and pepper and sugar to taste. Stir in chicken broth. Cook about 30 minutes or longer, until thick. Add mushrooms and olives and most of their liquid and cook down until thick, rich sauce is formed.

Cook, drain, and blanch large package of spaghetti. In casserole alternate spaghetti, chicken, and sauce, ending with sauce. Top with Parmesan or grated cheddar cheese. Bake at 350 degrees for 1 hour.

Carol adds a note about her dish: "You can use a canned chicken if you're in a hurry. There's plenty of broth in a whole canned chicken to go into the sauce. Be sure you have plenty of sauce for the amount of spaghetti you use so it doesn't get too dry when it bakes."

Carol (Mrs. Jimmy) Owens, Glendale, California

Carol Owens is one of those people who kind of "sparkles." She and her husband Jimmy, composer-arranger-conductor, have collaborated on two very successful Christian musicals, "Show Me" and "Come Together." (I have listened as one of the audience to the latter, and it is a most beautiful worship experience.) Jimmy has a whole list of records to his credit, including Word and Light albums, and is currently music director of "Treehouse Club" television program, of which I am hostess.

Hot Chicken Salad

My thanks to Mrs. Richard Nixon for this special recipe.

4 cups cold cut-up chicken chunks, cooked
2 tablespoons lemon juice
¾ cup mayonnaise
1 teaspoon salt
½ teaspoon monosodium glutamate
2 cups chopped celery
4 hard-boiled eggs, sliced
¾ cup condensed cream of chicken soup
1 teaspoon onion, finely minced
2 pimentos, cut fine
1 cup cheese, grated
1½ cups crushed potato chips
⅔ cup toasted almonds, finely chopped

Combine all ingredients except cheese, potato chips, and almonds. Place in a large rectangular dish. Top with cheese, potato chips, and almonds. Let stand overnight in refrigerator. Bake in 400-degree oven for 20 to 25 minutes. Serves 8.

Pat (Mrs. Richard) Nixon, San Clemente, California

Oven Chicken Salad for Six

2 cups cubed cooked chicken	1 cup mayonnaise
1 cup diced celery	½ cup milk or chicken broth
½ cup salted cashews	¼ cup pimento
3 tablespoons lemon juice	1 3½-oz. can French fried on-
½ cup chopped green pepper	ion rings
¼ teaspoon salt	Dash of paprika

Mix in order given, but reserve ½ can onion rings and paprika. Bake in greased 1½ quart casserole, covered, for 30 minutes at 350 degrees. Top with remaining onion rings and garnish with paprika. Bake 5 minutes more, uncovered.

Virginia (Mrs. D. Elton) Trueblood, Richmond, Indiana

Taking pictures and showing slides, knitting sweaters and mittens for grandchildren, and traveling and sightseeing are some of Virginia Trueblood's special interests. She mentions that her real interest is caring for her husband, Author and Lecturer D. Elton Trueblood.

Chicken-Almond Casserole

A rich and special chicken recipe you'll be proud to serve to dinner guests!

8 oz. macaroni or noodles	2 teaspoons Worcestershire
2 tablespoons butter	sauce
2 tablespoons minced onion	1 cup grated American cheese
1 cup thinly sliced celery	2 cups diced, cooked chicken
2 tablespoons flour	¼ cup chopped pimento
¼ teaspoon dry mustard	¼ cup green pepper
2½ teaspoons salt	1 small can mushrooms
⅛ teaspoon pepper	1 cup roasted almonds
2½ cups milk	½ cup buttered bread crumbs

Cook macaroni or noodles until almost tender; drain and

rinse with cold water. Melt butter in pan. Add onion and celery; cook and stir about 5 minutes. Blend in flour, mustard, salt, and pepper. Add milk and Worcestershire sauce, stirring constantly. Cook until smooth and thickened. Stir in cheese, chicken, pimento, green pepper, macaroni, mushrooms and half of the almonds.

Turn into shallow baking dish; sprinkle with crumbs and remaining almonds. Bake in 400-degree oven for 20 minutes until lightly browned on top. Dish can be prepared day before serving and stored in refrigerator. 10 to 12 servings.

Fern (Mrs. Art) Taylor, Grand Rapids, Michigan

Fern and Art Taylor are old friends from college days. In fact, Fern was "Aunt Fur" to our children for years when they were small. Art is pastor of Good Shepherd Church in Grand Rapids, Michigan.

DRAKE'S CHICKEN DELIGHT

The apricot marmalade creates a new and interesting flavor.

4 boned chicken breasts
1 envelope onion soup mix

1 12-oz. jar of apricot marmalade
1 12-oz. bottle Russian dressing

Lay chicken breasts in a 9-inch square casserole. Mix the next three ingredients together and pour this over the chicken. Cover with foil or lid. Bake at 350 degrees for one hour. Reduce heat to 300 degrees and bake for another 30 minutes.

Diane says, "I serve this succulent chicken with steamed rice or *al dente* green noodles."

Diane (Mrs. Vernon) Drake, Boca Raton, Florida

See Diane's Pork Chop Casserole recipe on page 32 and Plenty for Twenty on page 27.

CHICKEN CANTONESE

3 tablespoons vegetable oil
6 oz. fine egg noodles
4 chicken breasts, split in half
1 envelope of onion soup, dissolved in 1 cup water

2 tablespoons soy sauce
1 can water chestnuts, with liquid
1 10-oz. pkg. frozen green peas

Heat vegetable oil in skillet or casserole. Add noodles and sauté, stirring until golden brown (about 5 minutes). Place chicken in casserole over noodles. Pour onion soup over chicken. Add soy sauce and liquid from water chestnuts. Bake 1 hour at 350 degrees. Add thawed peas and sliced water chestnuts. Bake 10 minutes longer or until peas are tender.

Henrietta (Mrs. Louis) Sutera, Mansfield, Ohio

Louis Sutera is an identical twin to Ralph Sutera. Both Louis and Ralph are actively engaged in evangelistic crusades in the United States and Canada.

BUSY DAY CHICKEN BAKE

1¼ cups hash brown potatoes or "Tater Tots," frozen
1 teaspoon salt
⅛ to ¼ teaspoon cayenne or black pepper
1 frying chicken (1½ to 2½ lbs.) quartered or cut into 8 pieces
1 10½-oz. can condensed cream of mushroom soup

1⅓ cups water
½ cup sour cream
1 pkg. chicken gravy mix or 1 chicken bouillon cube, crushed
1 tablespoon instant minced onion
6 stuffed green olives, sliced
Paprika

Sprinkle dry potatoes over bottom of 13 x 9-inch baking dish. Mix salt and pepper and sprinkle over chicken pieces. Place chicken on potatoes. Blend soup with remaining ingredients except olives and paprika. Pour over chicken and potatoes. Sprinkle with sliced olives and paprika. Bake at 375 degrees for 45 to 50 minutes.

Helen (Mrs. Randy) Rominger, Frankfurt, Germany, and Banner Elk, North Carolina

Randy and Helen Rominger were so nice to me when I was in Germany recently. Although I only met them when I arrived, they treated me like an old friend. Randy is with the Air Force and is stationed in Frankfurt. We surely got a lot of sightseeing done together.

CURRIED BREASTS OF CHICKEN

6 chicken breasts
Flour
Paprika
Cooking oil
1 10½-oz. can condensed cream of chicken soup

1 teaspoon curry powder
½ cup chopped blanched almonds
½ cup sour cream

Dip chicken breasts in flour and paprika. Fry until golden brown. Then place breasts in baking pan. Cover with soup and curry. Bake, covered, for about 50 minutes at 350 degrees. Then add almonds and sour cream. Bake 10 minutes longer and make gravy with pan drippings. Serve with rice and peach halves stuffed with chutney and broiled. *Delicious!*

Ruth (Mrs. Johnnie) Hallett, Seal Beach, California

Ruth is the wife of composer, pianist, and conductor Johnnie Hallett, and has written some of the lyrics for Johnnie's songs. (One of the most popular is "Thank You, Jesus.") Ruth says she loves living is California (So do I, Ruth!), after living most of her life in the East, and enjoys her work as a beauty consultant for Mary Kay Cosmetics. The Hallets have a French poodle named—appropriately—"Maestro."

June's Chicken Casserole

¾ cup rice, uncooked
4 tablespoons butter, melted
2 10½-oz. cans condensed
cream of chicken soup
1 10½-oz. can condensed
cream of mushroom soup

1 10½-oz. can condensed
cream of celery soup
Salt and pepper to taste
4 chicken breasts, whole
Mayonnaise

Mix rice, butter, soups, and salt and pepper to taste. Pour into 9x13-inch low baking dish. Split 4 breasts of chicken. Spread tops with light coating of mayonnaise and place on top of soup mixture. Bake at 325 degrees for 2 hours.

June (Mrs. Paul) Andersen, Trumbull, Connecticut

Pastor and Mrs. Andersen have spent a happy twenty-five years working in their beautifully picturesque Evangelical Free Church in Trumbull, Connecticut. (I've had the pleasure of singing there more than once.) Among her other talents, June is a very clever interior decorator. The Andersens are new grandparents, and enjoy traveling as a hobby.

Sunday Yum Yum

Colleen Evans says this dish can be "built" a day ahead and put in the oven after Sunday church for a quick dinner. (The name makes it almost irresistible!)

6 chicken breasts, split and
boned
6 slices ham, sliced ¼-inch
thick

1 pkg. frozen broccoli spears
Your favorite nippy cheese
sauce

Stew chicken until tender. Put precooked ham slices in bottom of glass baking pan. Place chicken breasts on top of ham. Cook and season broccoli and place on top of chicken. Pour cheese sauce over all. Cover with foil and refrigerate until you are ready to bake it. Bake in 375-degree oven for ½ hour until cheese sauce is bubbly and looks done. Serve with salad and rolls.

Colleen (Mrs. Louis H., Jr.) Evans, Washington, D.C.

Colleen Townsend Evans is a name well known in the Christian field. Former actress and Hollywood personality, Colleen is married to Louis H. Evans, Jr., pastor of National Presbyterian Church. She has listed under "Special interests"— "life, family, neat husband, four teen-age children." She also enjoys taking part in church projects, and her brand new interest is writing.

Six-Can Casserole

Okay, chefs, get out your trusty can opener and zip your way to happiness!

2 small cans of chicken
1 10½-oz. can condensed cream of celery soup
1 10½-oz. can condensed cream of mushroom soup

1 4-oz. can mushrooms, drained
1 cup diced celery
1 can chow mein noodles

Combine all ingredients except noodles and pour into buttered casserole. Before placing in oven, sprinkle noodles on top of casserole. Bake in preheated 325-degree oven for 1 hour. Serves 4 or 5.

Doris (Mrs. George) Gardiner, Grand Rapids, Michigan

Doris Gardiner sent several recipes, but I liked this one because it's speedy and easy. The Gardiners have three grown children and are proud grandparents as well. George Gardiner is the busy pastor of Calvary Undenominational Church in Grand Rapids, Michigan.

Viva la Chicken Tortilla Casserole

Olé! *Just wanted to get the attention of all you Spanish food lovers. When I read this title, I felt like singing "La Cucaracha." (Or something Spanish in better taste!) I can almost hear great crowds of people shouting: Viva la Chicken Tortilla Casserole!*

4 whole chicken breasts
1 dozen corn tortillas
1 10½-oz. can condensed
cream of chicken soup
1 10½-oz. can condensed
cream of mushroom soup

1 cup milk
2 tablespoons instant minced
onion
1 8-oz. can green chile salsa-
ortega
1 lb. cheddar cheese, grated

Wrap chicken breasts in foil and bake 1 hour at 400 degrees, or until tender. Bone and cut into large pieces. Cut tortillas into one-inch squares. Mix soups, milk, onion, and salsa.

Grease large shallow baking dish. Place tablespoon or two of water in bottom. Place layer of tortillas, chicken, soup mixture, and cheese. Continue until you have three layers ending with soup and cheese. Cover with foil and refrigerate 24 hours. Bake at 300 degrees for 1–1½ hours.

Nell (Mrs. John) Wooden, Santa Monica, California

Nell and her husband, John, are proud grandparents of seven. John is former basketball coach at UCLA and author of They Call Me Coach *published by Word Books. Nell writes that her special interests include her family first of all, and playing golf once a week.*

Chipped Beef 'n' Chicken

Here's a simple but tasty way to fix that good ol' standby— chicken. Definitely company fare, so get out the china!

1 pkg. chipped beef
Chicken breasts
Bacon slices

1 10½-oz. can condensed
cream of mushroom soup
1 cup sour cream

Line glass baking dish with small pieces of chipped beef. Bone chicken breasts. Wrap a piece of bacon around each rolled breast. Arrange in dish. Combine soup and sour cream and pour over top. Cover with plastic wrap and marinate overnight.

Bake *uncovered* 3 hours in slow 275-degree oven. Serve with wild rice.

Mary (Mrs. Ward) Oury, Wheaton, Illinois

Mary leads a very active life, being chauffeur for her newspaperman husband, working as a secretary, and studying stenotype in her spare time.

TURKEY SALAD BAKE

2 cups finely crushed potato chips (4-oz. pkg.)
½ cup grated sharp cheddar cheese (or Monterey Jack, Swiss)
½ cup chopped walnuts
1 tablespoon butter

2 cups cubed cooked turkey
2 cups thinly sliced celery
2 teaspoons grated onion
¼ teaspoon salt
2 tablespoons lemon juice
½ cup mayonnaise

Mix potato chips and cheese in small bowl. Pat half of mixture into bottom of shallow baking dish. Reserve remainder for topping.

Sauté walnuts in butter in small frying pan, stirring often, for 15 minutes or until lightly toasted. Drain on paper toweling. Toss with remaining ingredients. Spoon into prepared baking dish. Sprinkle remaining potato chip mixture on top. Bake in preheated oven at 450 degrees for 10 minutes, or until hot and golden.

Freda (Mrs. Henry) Teichrob, Regina, Saskatchewan, Canada

Freda and Henry Teichrob have opened their home to me

several times when I was in Regina. They head the counseling program for the Sutera's city-wide evangelistic campaigns and are seeing exciting things happen.

CREAMED TURKEY ON BISCUITS

Not quite a casserole, but you're gonna love this one the week after Thanksgiving! (P.S. It's a "Mim original.")

1 envelope onion soup	6 tablespoons flour
3 cups turkey broth or part turkey gravy	2 tablespoons sugar
1 cup diced celery	Salt and pepper to taste
1 onion, chopped medium fine	4 cups cooked chopped turkey pieces
4 tablespoons butter or margarine	Homemade biscuits

Cook together over medium heat soup mix, turkey broth, celery, and onion until celery is done. Make soft paste of butter and flour over low heat. Mix slowly about a cup of the hot broth mixture into the butter and flour paste (and watch out for lumps!). Combine slowly with the remainder of the hot liquid, stirring well.

Add sugar and then add salt and pepper to taste. Continue to cook for about 15 minutes over low heat. Add chopped turkey and cook for a short while for the turkey to heat. Serve over homemade biscuits or rice. Will serve 4 or more depending on size of portions.

Mim (Mrs. Bob) Brooks, Ft. Lauderdale, Florida

Mim is quite a clever gal and has made all her own clothes since she was twelve. She is also an artist and enjoys being an amateur photographer. Her husband, Bob, was music director at Coral Ridge Presbyterian Church for several years and is a very talented arranger and conductor. The Brookses have two teen-age daughters and a "delightful" dog. (That's a direct quote from Mim!)

TURKEY-RICE CASSEROLE

How about that leftover turkey? After three nights of trying to disguise it, your husband might appreciate this one! Ruth says it's also nice for a church or school supper.

1 10½-oz can condensed
   cream of celery soup
2 cups water
1 teaspoon salt
¼ teaspoon Worcestershire
   sauce
Dash of pepper

1½ cups Minute Rice
1½ cups diced, cooked turkey
1½ cups cooked peas
2-3 tablespoons diced pimento
2 tablespoons coarsely
   chopped parsley

Combine soup, water, salt, Worcestershire sauce, and pepper in saucepan; bring to a boil over medium heat. Remove from heat and add remaining ingredients. Pour into 2-quart buttered casserole. Heat in oven for about 15 minutes at 400 degrees.

Ruth (Mrs. Thomas) McDill, Minneapolis, Minnesota

Ruth says she still finds being a pastor's wife the most interesting kind of life. She assists in a nursery school and is active in the Women's Fellowship of the National Association of Evangelicals.

Vegetables

DEAR FATHER,
Let my soul use Thy
    love and grace
To the fullest,
That it may remain lean
    and hungry
For the food that only my
    Master
Can provide.
Let it come starving
To receive the Bread of Life.
Let it come parched and dry
To drink of Thy love.

As my body burns its engery
    to leanness
In use of its nourishment,
So let my soul in service
    to Thee.

                    Amen.

                                Lois Fiedler

Asparagus Casserole Superb

This one is surely company fare!

3 eggs, hard-cooked	Dash of pepper
¼ cup butter	½ cup grated cheddar cheese
¼ cup flour	2 cans asparagus spears
1 cup milk	1 can water chestnuts
½ teaspoon salt	⅔ cup bread crumbs

Cool, peel, and slice hard-cooked eggs. Make cream sauce of butter, flour, milk, salt, and pepper. Cook till thickened. Stir in grated cheddar cheese. Place drained asparagus in oblong shallow casserole. Top with thinly sliced water chestnuts, then egg slices. Pour sauce over all. Sprinkle lightly with bread crumbs. Bake at 350 degrees for 20–25 minutes. Serves 8–10.

Betty (Mrs. Warren) Wiersbe, Chicago, Illinois

Betty Wiersbe sent two recipes I thought you'd enjoy, so I'm delighted to feature both of them. The other recipe is Spoon Bread on page 112.

Betty's husband, Warren Wiersbe, is the author of several books and the pastor of Moody Church in Chicago. Betty keeps busy with her duties as a mother and pastor's wife.

Green Beans Parmesan

1 lb. green beans	1½ to 2 tablespoons butter
1 cup water	Slivered almonds
1 pkg. onion soup mix	Parmesan cheese

Cook beans, water, and soup mix together for about 40 minutes. Drain, pour into casserole, and add butter. Mix almonds through beans and sprinkle cheese on top.

Ruth Leonard, Valparaiso, Indiana

Green's Bean Casserole

3 cans French-style green
  beans, drained

1 10½-oz. can condensed
  cream of mushroom soup
2 cans fried onion rings

Moisten string beans with can of mushroom soup. Bake in
oven at 350 degrees for 10 minutes. Take out and sprinkle one
can of onion rings on top and bake for 5 more minutes. Take
out and sprinkle remainder of onion rings on top. Keep warm
until serving.

Anita Bryant (Mrs. Bob) Green, Miami Beach, Florida

*Recording artist, performer, television personality, wife, and
mother of four, Anita Bryant Green seems to do them all well.
(And believe me, I know it's not easy.) Anita is married to
Bob Green who has his own production company in Miami
Beach, Bob Green Productions, Inc. This is Anita's recipe for
Green's Bean Casserole. (That's hard to say!)*

Glorified Beans

1½ lbs. ground beef
1½ cups chopped onions
1 tablespoon dried mixed
  peppers
1¼ teaspoons salt
2 tablespoons brown sugar
1 tablespoon chili powder

1 12-oz. can tomato paste
1 cup water
1 can pork and beans in tomato sauce
1 can green limas
1 can red kidney beans

Brown ground beef. Combine with rest of ingredients and
bake at 350 degrees for 1 hour. Serves 6.

Adele (Mrs. Richard) Carmichael, Glendale, California

*Besides being the mother of Ruth Adele Martin and Ralph
Carmichael, Adele Carmichael is quite a woman. (Ralph's
wife, Mar, says she does everything well!) She not only teaches*

four to five Bible classes a week, but she also finds time to sew, paint china, paint pictures, and crochet cute hats. (I know —I have one!)

HAM AND BEANS CASSEROLE

"This is my own version of New England Baked Beans," writes Mary Frances Fickett. "When served with a generous plate of fresh California fruit slices and hot Texas biscuits, topped off with American apple pie and ice cream, you can make a preacher's family pretty happy!"

1 large can of New England baked beans	½ cup maple syrup
1 cup of baked ham, cut in pieces	¼ cup chopped white onion

Combine all ingredients and bake 1 hour in moderate oven, 325 to 350 degrees.

Mary Frances (Mrs. Harold) Fickett, Barrington, Rhode Island

And that's just what Mrs. Fickett does—makes a preacher's family happy! Her husband, Harold Fickett, Jr., was pastor of the well known First Baptist Church of Van Nuys, California, and is now President of Barrington College, Barrington, Rhode Island.

BROCCOLI CASSEROLE

1 pkg. frozen broccoli	4 eggs, separated
2 cups heavy white sauce	½ teaspoon nutmeg
Parmesan cheese	

Purée broccoli. Make white sauce and add Parmesan cheese and broccoli. Beat 4 egg yolks and add to mixture. Beat egg whites; then fold egg whites and nutmeg into mixture. Pour into casserole. Set baking pan or casserole in water. Bake at 350 degrees for 40 minutes.

Martha (Mrs. Charlie) Shedd, Oxnard, California

Martha is the wife of Charlie Shedd, minister and author of many books, among them The Stork Is Dead, Promises to Peter, and The Fat Is in Your Head, published by Word Books. Martha likes to cook and does rug-braiding and knitting in her spare time. She takes pleasure in helping her husband with his books and in preparing radio talks, which are taped monthly.

BROCCOLI-MUSHROOM CASSEROLE

1 chopped onion
Margarine
3 pkgs. frozen broccoli spears
1 medium can mushrooms
2 10½-oz. cans condensed
   cream of mushroom soup

1 pkg. garlic cheese
1 teaspoon monosodium glutamate
½ cup slivered almonds
1 cup bread crumbs

Sauté onion until tender. Cook frozen broccoli until tender. Combine onions and broccoli with mushrooms, mushroom soup, garlic cheese, monosodium glutamate, and mix thoroughly. Add ¾ of the almonds. Continue to mix thoroughly. Cover with bread crumbs and remainder of almonds, and bake at 350 degrees until bubbly.

Shirley (Mrs. Pat) Boone, Beverly Hills, California

Shirley Boone took time out from a hectic schedule "on the road" with her husband, Pat, and four lovely daughters to share this luscious Broccoli Casserole. Shirley has now turned author, and her book One Woman's Liberation, Creation House, is sure to be a best seller.

BROCCOLI DIVINE

1 cup chopped celery
1 cup chopped onions
2-3 tablespoons margarine
1 small jar Cheese Whiz

1 10½-oz. can condensed
  cream of chicken soup
2 pkgs. frozen broccoli cuts,
  cooked according to directions
2 cups cooked rice

Sauté celery and onions in margarine. Stir in cheese and soup. Add this sauce to broccoli and rice which have been mixed together. Pour into greased casserole and bake at 350 degrees for 30 minutes.

Doris (Mrs. Gordon) Dorian, Wichita, Kansas

Doris and her husband, Pastor Gordon Dorian, are in the nineteenth year of their pastorate at Olivet Church in Wichita, Kansas. I had the pleasure of staying with this delightful family when I sang in their church a few years ago.

SCALLOPED CABBAGE

Jean advises: "For a main dish, try this delicious variation: Add ½ can corned beef to each layer."

4 cups cooked cabbage
2 cups white sauce

Salt and pepper to taste
¼ cup buttered bread crumbs

Place layer of cooked cabbage in buttered casserole; cover with white sauce and season with salt and pepper to taste. Add second layer of cabbage and white sauce. Top with buttered bread crumbs. Do not cover. Bake at 375 degrees about 1 hour.

White sauce:
2 tablespoons melted butter
2 tablespoons flour

2 cups milk

Mix melted butter and flour. Stir in milk and cook until thickened.

Jean (Mrs. Henry) Walther, Denver, Colorado

Jean Walther has taught school for seventeen years and is now in training for Christian counseling. Her husband, Hank, is a microwave engineer.

CARROT CASSEROLE

This is a simple Pennsylvania Dutch recipe:

1 minced onion	2 eggs, slightly beaten
1 cup celery, finely cut	½ cup milk
3 tablespoons butter	1 teaspoon salt
3 cups cooked, mashed carrots	½ cup bread crumbs

Sauté onion and celery in butter and add to mashed carrots. Add rest of ingredients. Place mixture in buttered casserole and bake uncovered for 20–30 minutes at 350 degrees.

Lynne (Mrs. Wilmer) Hallman, Pottstown, Pennsylvania

Lynne is the mother of a five-year-old son, and her husband, Wil, is director and vice president of Pottstown Youth Centre, Inc. Wil's father, Stanley Hallman, is founder and director of this wonderful work, which has been helping youth for many years in the Pottstown area. Both Lynne and Wil sing with a talented group of young people called "The Image Singers." See Lynne's other recipe on page 88—Ratatouille.

CAULIFLOWER CASSEROLE DELUXE

1 medium head (or 2 boxes frozen) cauliflower	2 cups milk
¼ cup diced green pepper	1 teaspoon salt
	1 6-oz. can broiled mushrooms

¼ cup butter | 6 slices pimento cheese
¼ cup flour | Paprika

Separate cauliflower and cook in salted water until tender 10–15 minutes. Drain. Cook green pepper in melted butter. Blend in flour. Stir in milk, stirring constantly until thick. Add salt and mushrooms.

Place ½ the cauliflower in 1½-quart casserole. Cover with ½ the cheese, then ½ the sauce. Repeat layers. Sprinkle top with paprika. Brown lightly in 350-degree oven about 15 minutes. (If prepared ahead of time, bake a little longer.)

Frances (Mrs. Harry) Gommoll, Media, Pennsylvania

Fran is the wife of a Methodist minister, grandmother of two "great little boys" (Grandma's exact words!), and has been church organist and choir director "at various times." She was also my husband's secretary back in Pennsylvania days and is a great gal. In those days, we shamelessly referred to her as "Gommy" because of her unusual last name. (I think she still might be looking for a way to get even. Maybe that's why she sent two recipes!) Her other recipe, Country Noodle Casserole, is on page 103.

COMPANY CORN CUSTARD

2½ cups milk | 4 eggs
2 tablespoons butter or margarine | ½ teaspoon salt
1 17-oz. can cream-style corn | ¼ cup sugar

Heat milk to boiling point. Melt butter in heavy pan; add corn and allow to heat slowly till warm through. Beat eggs slightly till thoroughly mixed; add salt and sugar and then corn. Place in 2½-quart casserole and add hot milk. Stir, then bake at 350 degrees in preheated oven for 30 to 35 minutes or until center starts to thicken. Do not overbake and it will be smooth and creamy—never watery.

Phyllis (Mrs. Arthur L.) Michael, Shickshinny, Pennsylvania

Phyllis Michael is well known as a poet and hymn writer and loves teaching music to children. She has written five books and has biographical sketches in several publications, among them Who's Who of American Women.

CORN CASSEROLE

Lovely and talented television personality-recording artist, Norma Zimmer is also a very gracious lady who is nice to be around. Wife and mother as well, Norma writes that this recipe is an old family standby.

1 No. 2 can cream-style corn	2 eggs, beaten
1 No. 2 can tomatoes	⅓ cup sliced pimento
½ cup yellow corn meal	Stuffed olives
1 cup milk	Salt and pepper to taste
1 tablespoon melted butter	Dry bread crumbs
1 small onion, chopped	Butter

Combine all ingredients except bread crumbs and final butter and pour into greased casserole. Add dry bread crumbs to top. Dot with butter and bake at 350 degrees for 1½ hours.

Norma (Mrs. Randy) Zimmer, LaHabra, California

RATATOUILLE

Lynne said her Aunt Jane handed down this authentic French recipe to her. (I think it's the only recipe I received involving eggplant, a tasty vegetable but not very well known.)

1 large eggplant	Onion
Salt	Green pepper

| 1 large zucchini squash | Tomatoes (juiced and |
| Olive oil | seeded) |

Peel and slice eggplant. Salt each slice and let stand in a bowl with weight on top to remove juice for at least ½ hour. Follow same procedure with zucchini squash. Wash salt off and dry each piece of eggplant and squash. Sauté in olive oil until tender. Add onion, green pepper, and tomatoes (to taste) and cook the whole mixture until most of the juices are evaporated. Place in buttered casserole or baking dish and bake for 20 minutes at 350–375 degrees.

Lynne (Mrs. Wilmer) Hallman, Pottstown, Pennsylvania

Lynne sent two casserole recipes, this sophisticated one and a simple Pennsylvania Dutch recipe, Carrot Casserole, on page 86.

POTATO CASSEROLE

A delightful Pennsylvania Dutch recipe from Anna Myrl Long:

1 egg, beaten	4 cups bread, cubed
2 cups mashed potatoes	1 teaspoon poultry seasoning
2 tablespoons butter	1 tablespoon minced parsley
1 onion, chopped	1 teaspoon salt
½ cup celery, diced	Dash of pepper

Put the beaten egg into the mashed potatoes and mix well. Melt the butter in a large skillet and sauté the onion and celery. Stir in bread cubes to toast for a few minutes, stirring constantly. Add all other ingredients, combine with potatoes, and mix thoroughly. Put in buttered casserole, dot with butter, and bake in moderate oven until lightly browned.

This dish is very delicious with turkey or chicken—especially at Thanksgiving or Christmas time.

Anna Myrl (Mrs. Stan) Long, Upland, California

See Anna Myrl Long's other Pennsylvania Dutch recipe, Stuffed Peppers, on page 22.

SAVORY SCALLOPED CHEESE POTATOES

Here's a recipe for good ol' scalloped potatoes with a nice "cheesy" touch. You can also add ham if you want to "beef" it up a little. (Ham it up??)

4 large or 6 medium potatoes
2 cups diced ham (optional and good without)
1/4 cup butter
1/2 lb. cheddar cheese or more
1 cup minced onions

1/2 cup minced parsley
1 tablespoon salt
1 teaspoon pepper
1 teaspoon paprika to redden each layer
2 1/2 cups half and half and milk

Butter bottom and sides of 12 x 8 x 2-inch baking dish. Wash, peel, and slice thin 4 large or 6 medium potatoes. Put in ice water for 10 to 15 minutes; drain. Put layer of potatoes (and ham) into dish, dot with butter, sprinkle thickly with sharp shredded cheddar cheese, finely minced onions, parsley, salt, pepper, and paprika. Do this until you have four layers.

Save 1/4 cup of cheese for top of dish. Pour about 2 1/2 cups of half and half and milk over layers, enough to cover. Bake in 450-degree oven for 10 minutes. Reduce to 350 degrees; sprinkle on 1/4 cup of cheese and bake at least 2 hours.

Vera (Mrs. Cy) Jackson, Los Angeles, California

Two very "easy to like" people are Vera and Cy Jackson. Vera is with the National Automobile Club of North Hollywood, and Cy is West Coast regional marketing manager for Word, Inc.

Sweet Potato Pudding

1 medium size pan of sweet potatoes	1 small can evaporated milk
1 cup sugar	Pinch of salt
2 eggs	Marshmallows
	Nutmeg

Cook potatoes and mash. Add sugar, eggs, milk, and salt. Place in casserole. Arrange marshmallows on top and sprinkle with nutmeg. Bake slowly until heated through and marshmallows are nicely browned.

Grace (Mrs. Lester) Place, Spring City, Pennsylvania

Grace and Lester Place, musical evangelists, have had a rich ministry traveling throughout the United States and Canada for thirty-two years. Our paths have crossed now and then, and it's always a delight to see them.

Mushroom and Rice Casserole

3½ large onions, chopped	2 10½-oz. cans consomme soup
⅔ lb. butter	2 cans water
1 large can mushrooms (in butter)	2 cups Uncle Ben's raw rice
	Salt to taste (about 2 tsp.)

Sauté onions in butter; then add mushrooms and sauté for a few minutes. Mix all ingredients together and place in one large casserole or two small ones. Cover with top of dish or aluminum foil and bake at 350 degrees for 2 hours. Be sure to stir after 1 hour.

Mavis (Mrs. Bill) Glass, Duncanville, Texas

Mavis Glass says she "loves to cook" for her husband and three children, and also enjoys needlepoint and "fiddling with our brood mares." Her husband, Bill, was an all-pro defensive end for the Cleveland Browns for ten years. (I said that right, didn't I??!) Bill Glass now holds city-wide evangelistic campaigns and is the author of several books, My Greatest Challenge, Stand Tall and Straight, Get in the Game, *and his latest,* Don't Blame the Game, *published by Word Books.*

SPINACH AND RICE CASSEROLE

Vonette Bright says this casserole is good as a main dish for vegetarians. She also serves it often when entertaining guests from India.

1 pkg. frozen spinach, cooked and drained
1 lb. sharp cheddar cheese, grated
1 cup milk
4 eggs, beaten
1 tablespoon onion, finely chopped
1 tablespoon Worcestershire sauce
2 teaspoons salt
¼ teaspoon each thyme, rosemary, marjoram
¼ cup melted butter
3 cups cooked rice

Mix all together and bake in a 2-quart casserole set in pan of hot water. Bake 1 hour and 15 minutes at 350 degrees. Serves 8 as main dish, 16 as a vegetable.

Vonette (Mrs. Bill) Bright, Arrowhead Springs, California

Vonette Bright is the wife of Bill Bright, founder and president of Campus Crusade for Christ International. She devotes much time to speaking for various civic, church, and women's groups. Presently, she is actively engaged in organizing the Great Commission Prayer Crusade, uniting several thousand women across the nation to pray for a moral and spiritual awakening in our country.

Squash and Water Chestnut Casserole

2 cups yellow squash, cooked almost tender and drained
1 cup condensed cream of mushroom soup
¼ pack saltines, crushed (sometimes I don't use quite ¼ lb.)
4 tablespoons (½ stick) melted margarine

Black pepper to taste
½ cup water chestnuts, sliced thin
1 tablespoon minced onion flakes
Dash of Worcestershire sauce
1 tablespoon chopped red pimento (for color)
Grated cheese

Combine all ingredients except grated cheese. If this mixture seems to be too thick, add a little milk. Pour into buttered pan and bake about 20 minutes at 350 degrees. Just before taking out of oven, sprinkle grated cheese of your choice on top. Serves 6.

Editor's note: Dorothy says to "go light on salt" because the crackers and soup make it salty enough for her taste.

Dorothy (Mrs. Donnie) Royal, Salemburg, North Carolina

Dorothy Royal, besides being a good cook, is director of a boys choir, which I imagine can be verrry interesting at times!

Stuffed Acorn Squash

This is an "original" Jean dreamed up one cold evening after a day of apple picking and squash gathering.

2 acorn squash
1 10-oz. pkg. of chopped spinach, frozen
Chopped onion

1 4-oz. can mushrooms
1 cup shredded cheese, Swiss or sharp cheddar

Split squash and remove seeds. Place cut side down in flat

pan filled with ¼-inch boiling water. Bake at 350 degrees for 45 minutes.

Cook spinach flavored with chopped onion (to taste). Drain and add mushrooms and cheese. Toss gently, place in squash cavities, and return to oven for 15 minutes or until cheese is completely melted. Remove and serve on individual plates with a large Waldorf salad or tossed salad. Serves 4.

Jean (Mrs. Joe) Feiler, Chicago, Illinois

Mother of four children, vivacious Jean Feiler says that some of her most rewarding years were spent when she and her husband Joe were engaged in inner-city work in Chicago. The Feilers are people who believe in putting "teeth" into their Christianity, and reaching out to help others. Jean is now receptionist-secretary for the North Shore Baptist Church in Chicago.

TURKISH SQUASH

6 small yellow squashes
6 tablespoons (¾ stick) butter or margarine
2 cups saltine-cracker crumbs
1 large onion, chopped (1 cup)

1 cup (8-ounce carton) plain yogurt
2 tablespoons lemon juice
1 teaspoon salt
1 teaspoon crushed coriander
¼ teaspoon seasoned pepper

Halve squashes lengthwise; cook in boiling salted water in a large frying pan 10 minutes; lift out carefully; drain pan. Scoop out centers of squash and chop; drain well. Place shells in a shallow buttered pan.

Melt butter or margarine in same frying pan; toss 3 tablespoonsful of butter with 1 cup of the cracker crumbs in a small bowl. Add onion to butter in pan; sauté until soft; stir in remaining crumbs, chopped squash, and all remaining ingredients (except buttered crumbs). Spoon into shells. Sprinkle with buttered crumbs. Bake in moderate oven, 350 degrees, 20 minutes. Makes 6 servings.

SQUASH CASSEROLE

What a lovely way to fix squash, and so easy too! "This is delicious."

4 tablespoons (½ stick) butter	1 small onion, grated
4 oz. stuffing mix	½ 10½-oz. can condensed cream of chicken soup
1 box frozen squash, thawed	½ cup sour cream

Melt butter and mix with stuffing. Mix other ingredients and layer alternately with stuffing mix in casserole. Bake at 350 degrees for 30 minutes.

Hulda (Mrs. William) Jelley, Fayetteville, Pennsylvania

Hulda enjoys gardening and sewing for her grandchildren. Hulda's husband, Bill, is a long-time friend from the record industry.

ZUCCHINI ITALIANO

Zucchini on the half shell, with garlic, hot sausage, and Parmesan cheese.

6 medium-size zucchini, halved lengthwise	⅓ cup flavored bread crumbs
½ lb. hot Italian sausages	¼ cup grated Parmesan cheese
1 small onion, chopped (¼ cup)	Small white onion rings (optional)
1 clove of garlic, crushed	

Cook zucchini in boiling salted water in a large frying pan 10 minutes; lift out carefully; drain pan. Scoop out insides of zucchini and mash; drain well. Place shells in a shallow pan.

Peel casings from sausages; break up meat; sauté in same frying pan 5 minutes. Stir in onion and garlic; sauté until onion is soft. Stir in mashed zucchini and bread crumbs. Spoon into shells; sprinkle with cheese. Bake in moderate oven, 350 degrees, 30 minutes, or until heated through. Garnish with small white onion rings, if you wish. Serves 6.

ZUCCHINI SUMMER SPECIAL

3 green tomatoes, sliced thin	Pinch of oregano
1 large zucchini squash, sliced a little thicker	Pinch of salt
	Cooking oil
2 onions, sliced thin	

Simmer above ingredients in oil until tender. Pour into casserole. (Should fill it 9/10 full.)

1 can tomatoes	Pinch of garlic
1 tablespoon Hungarian paprika	Sharp cheese, grated

Make sauce of tomatoes, paprika, and garlic and pour over casserole. Top with a layer of grated cheese and sprinkle with paprika. Heat in moderate oven, 325–350 degrees, until bubbly. Cool slightly. Very rich. Serve with plain rolls and meat, and fruit for dessert.

Lois Hoadley (Mrs. Robert) Dick, Newton, New Jersey

Lois Hoadley Dick is one of my favorite writers, and her articles can be found in most of the Christian publications. Lois has a friend who is Hungarian and has taught her to use paprika in her cooking. She says that this is not the "American stuff" but is pronounced "pop're-ka," and unless you pronounce it right, the casserole won't turn out! So where do you get Hungarian paprika? In a Grand Union grocery store at the seasoning counter, or at an import store, I am told. Lois sent me a sample in her letter and the fragrance can best be described as "zowie"!

Southern Tomato Casserole

1 cup brown sugar	½ cup water
¼ cup white sugar	Dash of salt
1 16-oz. can tomato purée	4 slices of bread

Combine all ingredients except bread in saucepan and boil 2 or 3 minutes. Break up bread and place in baking dish. Pour boiled mixture over the bread and bake at 350 degrees for 20–25 minutes.

Dorothy (Mrs. William) Miedema, Los Alamitos, California

Being a pastor's wife can be a very busy life filled with church suppers and lots of entertaining. Dorothy's husband, William Miedema, is pastor of one of Southern California's most progressive churches, El Dorado Park Community Church in Long Beach. Dorothy says: "We use this dish as an extra at many large dinners. It seems to go well with most main courses."

Spanish Tomato Cups

6 large firm ripe tomatoes	6 tablespoons process
1 6-oz. pkg. Spanish rice mix	cheese spread
Water	Sliced ripe olives (optional)
2 tablespoons butter or margarine	

Cut a thin slice from top of each tomato; scoop out insides into 2-cup measuring cup. (There should be 2 cups.) Place tomato cups in a shallow pan. Prepare rice mix with water, butter or margarine, and the 2 cups tomato pulp, following label directions. Spoon into tomato cups; top each with 1 tablespoon cheese spread. Bake in moderate oven, 350 degrees, 20 minutes, or until heated through. Garnish with sliced ripe olives, if you wish. Serves 6.

Miscellaneous

For a Friend

I don't believe I've ever thought to thank you, God, for this wonderful friend. But I do thank you for creating her and letting her enrich my life this way.

Thank you for all the years we've known each other and the confidences and hopes and troubles that we've shared.

Thank you for the understanding we bring to each other. For the patience we have with each other's faults; for the advice and even the scoldings we are able to give each other without either of us taking offense.

Thank you for the help we have been to each other—in this way, and so many more. Thank you that because of her I am a better, happier person, and that she has grown as a person too because of me.

Thank you that she would give me anything in her power— time, money, work, possessions, encouragement, sympathy— whatever my need. And that she knows I would be as quick to respond to whatever her needs might be.

Thank you that we can laugh together, cry together, rejoice together. And although we may not see each other for a long time, when we do come together it is always the same.

Lord, bless and keep her, this person you fashioned and filled with qualities that have meant so much to me. Lord, thank you for my friend.

Marjorie Holmes

CHEESE FONDUE

Use a straight-sided earthenware pot for preparation. Serves 4.

8 oz. natural Swiss cheese, diced into ½-inch cubes
8 oz. natural Gruyère cheese, diced into ½-inch cubes
3 tablespoons flour
1 clove garlic
2 cups milk
¼ cup heavy cream
Freshly ground black pepper
2 loaves Italian bread, cut into 1-inch cubes or
2 lbs. small shrimp, cooked, shelled, and deveined

Mix cheese and flour. Rub fondue pot with garlic and discard garlic. Heat milk and cream in pot until just simmering. Add cheese, one handful at a time, stirring with a wooden spoon until cheese is melted. Add pepper to taste. Keep hot over a burner. Spear bread cubes or shrimp on fondue fork or stick and swirl through the fondue.

FONDUE BOURGUIGNONNE

Use a metal fondue pot, narrower at the top than at the bottom to prevent fat from spattering. Fill pot with oil ⅓ full; heat until oil just starts to smoke. Keep hot over alcohol burner. Spear food on fondue forks and dip in the oil until sufficiently done, then into cold sauce. The following foods may be used: 1-inch cubes of tender beef, 1-inch cubes of boneless and skinless chicken breast, shelled and deveined raw shrimp, scallops, cocktail frankfurters, small meatballs, chicken livers, cherry tomatoes, small mushrooms. As sauces, serve: Béarnaise, hollandaise, horseradish, mustard, mayonnaise, catsup, or chutney.

CHILI RELLENO CASSEROLE (Meatless)

1 7-oz. can whole chilies (not hot)
1 lb. cheddar cheese (shredded)
1 lb. Jack cheese (shredded)
4 eggs, separated

1 13-oz. can evaporated milk
3 tablespoons flour
Salt and pepper to taste
2 8-oz. cans tomato sauce

Remove seeds from chilies and flatten half of them in bottom of greased casserole (should be a deep one). Cover with cheddar cheese. Put rest of chilies next and cover with Jack cheese. Beat egg whites and yolks separately. Add milk and flour to yolks; then add salt and pepper to taste. Fold in beaten egg whites and pour mixture over chilies and cheese. Bake covered at 325 degrees for 1 hour. Uncover, pour tomato sauce over, and bake ½ hour longer. Serves 6 to 8.

Harriett (Mrs. Floyd) Thatcher, Waco, Texas

Floyd Thatcher personally recommended his wife Harriett's Chili Relleno Casserole. And what better authority could we ask??! Many thanks to Harriett and to Floyd, who is vice president and executive editor of Word Books, Waco, Texas.

CORNED-BEEF-HASH QUICHE

Unbaked 9-inch pie shell
1 15-oz. can corned-beef hash
1 cup (4 oz.) shredded Swiss cheese
2 teaspoons flour

¼ teaspoon salt
Dash of nutmeg
2 eggs, beaten
1¼ cups milk

Bake pie shell in very hot oven, 450 degrees, 7 minutes. Turn oven temperature control to 325 degrees. Crumble hash into pie shell and top with cheese. Mix remaining ingredients and pour over top. Bake 35 minutes, or until set. Cool 25 minutes. Serves 6.

Country Noodle Casserole

Bacony-flavored and luscious with a little nip of horseradish and Tabasco . . .

½ lb. sliced bacon
1 1-lb. pkg. very fine egg noodles or vermicelli noodles
3 cups cottage cheese
3 cups sour cream
2 cloves garlic, crushed
2 onions, minced

2 tablespoons Worcestershire sauce
Dash Tabasco sauce
4 teaspoons salt
3 tablespoons prepared horse-radish
1 cup grated Parmesan cheese
Extra sour cream

Fry bacon until crisp. Drain on paper towels and crumble. Cook noodles in boiling salted water until just tender, *al dente*, according to package directions. Drain well.

Mix all remaining ingredients, except Parmesan cheese and extra sour cream, in a large bowl. Add noodles and bacon and toss with two forks until well mixed. Turn into a deep 3½-quart buttered casserole. Cover and bake in a moderate oven, 350 degrees, for 30–40 minutes or until heated through. Remove cover, sprinkle surface with ¼ cup Parmesan cheese, and broil until golden. Save remaining Parmesan cheese and sour cream to top each portion. Serves 12.

Frances (Mrs. Harry) Gommoll, Media, Pennsylvania

My friend Fran Gommoll sent two recipes that are so good I have to include them both. It was really kind of a dirty trick, Fran, because you know I have trouble with decisions! Her other recipe, Cauliflower Casserole Deluxe, is on page 86.

CHILI TEX

1 can chili and beans
1 cup chopped onions
1 can yellow hominy

1 can pitted ripe olives
Grated cheese (for layers and
for top)

Alternate layers of above ingredients in buttered casserole.
Top with remaining grated cheese. Bake in 350-degree oven
until onions are tender. Serve with corn chips and a salad.

Dale Evans (Mrs. Roy) Rogers, Apple Valley, California

*I met Roy and Dale Rogers when I sang at a benefit in
Apple Valley, California, three years ago, and what a delightful
couple they are! Besides being a busy wife, mother, and performer, Dale spends time sharing her faith with audiences all
across the country. In fact, this recipe was hastily written from
a motel in Nebraska!*

CHILI PIE PRONTO

2½ cups corn chips
1 onion, chopped

1 cup cheese, chopped
1 can chili, warm

Place 1½ cups corn chips in dish. Sprinkle chopped onion
and ½ cup cheese over corn chips and pour chili over entire
mixture. Top with remaining 1 cup corn chips and ½ cup
cheese. Bake at 350 degrees for 10 minutes.

**Judy (Mrs. Bruce) Barton, Omaha, Nebraska
(formerly Frankfurt, Germany)**

*Judy and Bruce Barton made me feel so at home when I was
in Germany recently. Bruce was stationed in Frankfurt with
the Air Force. I especially enjoyed bicycling with Judy on the
paths in the forest near their home.*

COTTAGE CHEESE ROAST

In these days when people are very concerned about nutrition, I was delighted to receive these meatless recipes from Mrs. Fagal. They looked so interesting, I've decided to print them both!

1 large onion, chopped	5 eggs, well beaten
½ cup margarine	4 cups cottage cheese
3 envelopes George Washington's Seasoning and Broth	1 cup walnuts, chopped
	4 cups Kellogg's Special K

Sauté onion in margarine, then add George Washington powder, eggs, and all other ingredients. Mix well. Bake 1 hour at 350 degrees in large greased casserole. Serves 10–12.

MOCK SALMON LOAF

½ cup peanut butter	1 teaspoon salt
1 cup tomato juice	2 eggs, beaten until frothy
2 tablespoons margarine	1 cup raw carrots, grated
2 tablespoons onion, chopped	1 cup toasted bread crumbs
2 tablespoons parsley	

Mix peanut butter and tomato juice. In margarine, sauté (don't brown) onions and parsley. Add salt, eggs, carrots, and crumbs. Mix. Bake in greased loaf pan 45 to 50 minutes at 350 degrees, or fry in patties.

Virginia (Mrs. Wm. A.) Fagal, Newbury Park, California

Pastor and Mrs. Fagal have conducted the "Faith for Today" television program faithfully for over twenty-five years. The program has the distinction of being the longest-running religious television program in the United States. It was my great pleasure to work with them recently on a program they called "Bright New World."

GARLIC GRITS

If you've never heard of "garlic grits," please don't feel left out. I hadn't either, but I'm told it's a delicious dish. (You are probably 'way out ahead on this subject if you live below the Mason-Dixon!)

1 cup grits	½ cup (1 stick) margarine
2 eggs	1 roll garlic cheese, cut in
Milk	small pieces

Cook grits according to package directions until thick. Beat 2 eggs, put them in a one-cup measure, and add enough milk to make one cup. Combine all ingredients and mix well. Pour into casserole and bake at 350 degrees until brown (about 30 minutes).

Patricia (Mrs. Ron) Owens, Houston, Texas

If you've ever heard Ron and Patricia Owens sing, you'll never forget it. Not only are they highly professional Christian performers, but they are skilled in teaching as well. I think the lovely spirit with which they sing is as important as their voices. Besides keeping busy making records for Word and singing in concerts throughout the U.S., Ron is helping his brother to manage the lovely Hotel Rosat in Chateau d'Oex, Switzerland, and hops back and forth between Houston and Switzerland.

ICE CREAM EGGS

Good buddy Doris says she sends this original recipe "with malice towards none and charity for all!" Remember folks, you read it here first.

6 eggs	¼ cup (½ stick) butter or
3-4 scoops vanilla ice cream	margarine
Salt and pepper to taste	

Separate the eggs. Beat whites until firm peaks are formed.

Beat yolks until creamy. Add ice cream and salt and pepper to yolks. Beat until smooth. Fold egg whites into yolk mixture. *Do not beat.*

In a large skillet or electric frying pan (300–325 degrees) melt butter or margarine. Turn egg mixture into pan. Cook over low heat, turning occasionally with large spatula until golden brown. Serve immediately. Serves 4.

Note from Doris: Good for breakfast with bacon or ham, or with baked beans and cheese for late supper.

Doris (Mrs. Ed) Steinhart, Holliston, Massachusetts

Doris and Ed Steinhart are two musicians who make you wish you had stayed home and practiced when you were a child. Besides all that talent, they're just great people. They have a musical ministry at Ruggles Street Baptist Church in Boston, Massachusetts.

MACARONI AND EGGS

1 cup milk and water (mostly milk)	1 heaping cup macaroni
1 onion	2 tablespoons butter
3 cloves	1 tablespoon flour
Piece of carrot	4 eggs

Put milk and water in saucepan. Add onion (into which cloves have been stuck) and carrot. When mixture boils, add macaroni. Let cook until tender. Drain, saving liquid.

In another saucepan, place butter and carefully add flour, making a smooth paste. Slowly stir in liquid from macaroni, making a smooth and thickened white sauce. Add macaroni and place in shallow baking dish. Break eggs on top and bake for 5 to 10 minutes.

Hazel (Mrs. John) Owens, Chateau d'Oex, Switzerland

It was my pleasure to meet Rev. and Mrs. John Owens in

the beautiful Hotel Rosat in Chateau d'Oex, Switzerland, when I was on a concert tour. They managed the hotel for many years and now, recently retired, live in a lovely chalet on the side of a mountain overlooking the tiny town of Chateau d'Oex. The days I spent at the Rosat are unforgettable. They have old-fashioned feather-beds that are absolutely luscious and make you feel as if you're sleeping in a cocoon! Stepping out on the balcony of your room early in the morning made the whole trip worthwhile. The scenery is indescribably breathtaking. The Swiss are very gracious people. (I was presented with an armful of beautiful flowers at the conclusion of our concert in the town hall.) Rev. and Mrs. Owens are no exception and have a gift for making you feel welcome and comfortable.

WALNUT FANTASIA

This one takes first prize for most unusual! A perfect "waker-upper" for faded appetites . . .

Uncle Ben's wild rice

Walnut Balls:
2 cups chopped walnuts
2 teaspoons salt
½ cup finely chopped onions
1 cup grated mild cheddar or
longhorn cheese
Sauce:
2 10½-oz. cans condensed
cream of mushroom soup
1 pint sour cream

2 tablespoons parsley,
chopped
2 eggs
2 cups bread crumbs
½ cup milk
Cooking oil

2 cups fresh mushrooms, sautéed in butter

First boil your rice according to directions on the box. Mix all the ingredients (except cooking oil) for the walnut balls together, form into one-inch balls, and brown lightly in oil. Put rice in the bottom of the casserole. Cover it with the walnut balls.

Mix ingredients for sauce together and spread over the whole thing. Bake at 350 degrees for 30 minutes. (One of the joys of this dish for the working person is that the walnut balls can be made ahead of time and frozen.)

Elizabeth O'Connor, Washington, D.C.

Elizabeth O'Connor is on the staff of The Church of The Saviour in Washington, D. C. She coordinates the administrative details of the church, spending time each week at some frontier of the church's life. Elizabeth says, "My special interest is helping the church to create those structures that will enable this people to be on an inward-outward journey. I teach classes on "Keeping a Journal" and "Meditation and Contemplative Prayer" in our School of Christian Living. When I have time, which is not very often, I like to write." She is the author of several books: Call to Commitment; Journey Inward, Journey Outward; Our Many Selves. *Her two latest,* Eighth Day of Creation *and* Search for Silence, *were published by Word Books.*

HOT FRUIT CASSEROLE

Here's a different and delicious dessert casserole donated by Doris Moody.

Arrange in casserole after draining *well:*

1 large can peach halves	1 large can pineapple rings
1 large can pear halves	1 can bing cherries (op-
1 large can apricot halves	tional)

Combine spices, butter, and sugar over low heat:

¼ teaspoon cinnamon	1 tablespoon curry powder
¼ teaspoon ground cloves	Chopped nuts (optional)
½ cup butter or margarine	Sour cream
⅔ cup light brown sugar	

Dab spices-butter-sugar mixture over fruit casserole. Seal with foil. Bake at 350 degrees for 1 hour. Sprinkle with chopped nuts (optional). Serve with sour cream.

Doris (Mrs. Jess) Moody, West Palm Beach, Florida

Doris has many and varied interests. Among a few of her past activities: writer of Southern Baptist Convention materials, religious television writer-director, dean of women for Palm Beach Atlantic College. This year she is serving as associate dean of student affairs. She also works with the single adults and median adults in her church. Doris has two children and is married to Dr. Jess Moody, pastor of First Baptist Church of West Palm Beach, Florida, and author of several books, among them A Drink at Joel's Place *and* The Jesus Freaks, *published by Word Books.*

HEAVENLY FRUIT SALAD
(24 hour salad)

1 cup miniature marshmallows
¼ cup juice from canned pineapple
1 cup diced pineapple

1 cup mandarin orange sections
1 cup banana slices
½ firm ripe papaya, diced

Pour pineapple juice on marshmallows. Let stand ½ hour. Add well-drained fruits to marshmallows and refrigerate.

Coconut cream sauce:
1 egg
1 tablespoon sugar
2 tablespoons coconut syrup
1½ tablespoons light cream

Juice from ½ lemon
½ cup heavy cream, whipped
Maraschino cherries, garnish

For the sauce, beat egg until light. Gradually add sugar, coconut syrup, light cream and lemon juice. Mix. Cook in double boiler until thick, stirring constantly. Cool and fold into whipped heavy cream. Pour over fruit mixture and mix lightly. Chill 24 hours. Do not freeze. Garnish with maraschino cherries. Serves 6.

Adele (Mrs. Richard) Carmichael, Glendale, California

If you are ready for Glorified Beans and Heavenly Fruit Salad all in one meal, turn to page 82 for Adele's other recipe. (You could always top it off with Angel Feathers, Coffee-time Desserts, *for dessert!)*

DILLY CASSEROLE BREAD

My mom (who is one of the better cooks in the world) bakes this bread in a casserole. I would say this recipe is a "dilly," but you'd never forgive me!

1 packet active dry yeast or 1 cake compressed yeast	1 tablespoon butter
¼ cup warm water	2 teaspoons dill seed
1 cup creamed cottage cheese	1 teaspoon salt
2 tablespoons sugar	¼ teaspoon soda
1 tablespoon minced onion or onion soup mix	1 unbeaten egg
	2¼ to 2½ cups flour

Dissolve yeast in warm water. Combine cottage cheese, sugar, onion, butter, dill seed, salt, soda, egg, and yeast. Add flour a portion at a time to form a stiff dough, beating well after each addition. (For first addition of flour, use mixer on medium speed.) Cover and let rise in warm place until light and doubled in size, about 50–60 minutes.

Stir down dough. Turn into well-greased 8-inch round 1½- to 2-quart casserole. Let rise in warm place until light, 30 to 40 minutes. Bake at 350 degrees for 40 to 50 minutes until golden brown. Brush with soft butter and sprinkle with salt.

You can bake this bread early in the day and still serve it

warm at dinner time by wrapping it in aluminum foil and placing it in a 350-degree oven for about 15 minutes.

Theressa (Mrs. Raymond) Kleeves, Ludington, Michigan

SPOON BREAD

Spoon Bread is kind of a Southern specialty that even we Northern girls can enjoy!

1 cup boiling water
½ cup white corn meal
½ cup milk
½ teaspoon salt

1 tablespoon butter
1½ teaspoons baking powder
2 eggs, well beaten

Pour boiling water over white corn meal. Beat in milk, salt, butter, baking powder, and eggs. Pour into buttered 1-quart casserole. Bake until set at 400 degrees for 20–25 minutes. Serve hot with butter. 6 servings.

Betty (Mrs. Warren) Wiersbe, Chicago, Illinois

Betty Wiersbe sent two recipes I thought you'd enjoy, so I'm delighted to feature both of them. The other recipe is Asparagus Casserole Superb on page 81.

INDEX

Other quality cookbooks from WORD BOOKS

COFFEE-TIME DESSERTS
By Flo Price

Contains over 100 exciting family-tested recipes for all kinds of desserts for whatever time of day you need them . . . that chatty and relaxing morning coffee . . . the midafternoon pick-up . . . with dinner . . . that final midnight snack. The recipes are gathered from such outstanding Christian women as Mrs. Ralph Carmichael and Mrs. Billy Graham by Flo Price, who adds her own chatty comments. You can use these recipes with perfect confidence for formal and informal occasions alike, and you don't have to be a professional chef to get perfect results. Illustrated, indexed, spiral bound. #80083

FOOD FOR FELLOWSHIP COOKBOOK
By Antoinette Kuzmanich Hatfield

Mrs. Hatfield, wife of Oregon Senator Mark O. Hatfield, shares not only a choice collection of prized recipes of her own and her close friends but also her imaginative menus along with invaluable suggestions on how to be a perfect hostess. Recipes are arranged into 24 sections of around-the-clock occasions for church fellowship, and are easily adaptable for civic and community functions or private at-home entertaining. Illustrated, indexed. #80257

DAVID WADE'S MAGIC KITCHEN
By David Wade

The master sorcerer of food preparation shares his culinary know-how in a collection of outstanding recipes in all categories: salads, meats, seafood, vegetables, desserts, breads, appetizers. There is also an exciting selection from Mr. Wade's syndicated newspaper columns, with colorful historical background information on the recipes and their ingredients; a special group of non-alcoholic beverages for festive occasions; and some highly practical household helps. #80407

THE SPICE OF LIFE COOKBOOK

By David Wade

An heirloom treasury of tested recipes for the homemaker by internationally known gourmet David Wade. Beautiful inspirational poetry and thoughts that will enrich time spent in the kitchen enhance this collection of attractive recipes for every part of the well-planned menu. Simple, easy-to-follow directions help you create dishes that are elegant, yet suited to the average home and budget.   #80401

COOKING WITH A FLAIR

By David Wade

The best of David Wade. Crowning 20 years of culinary expertise—including nine previous cookbooks, numerous TV and radio programs (among them David's popular nationally syndicated TV show "The Gourmet"), magazine and newspaper features and personal demonstrations—David Wade offers his most popular, all-time favorite recipes in one book! Here, from the winner of the National Culinary Arts Society's top award for achievement in the food world, are recipes for those fabulous dishes that delighted you in a restaurant or at an impressive dinner party, plus valuable pointers for creating them in your own setting.   #80422